GW00393150

Ancilla to The Pre-Socratic Philosophers

A complete translation of the Fragments in Diels,
Fragmente der Vorsokratiker

by

Kathleen Freeman
D.LITT.

Author of *Companion to the Pre-Socratic Philosophers*, etc.

Oxford · Basil Blackwell
1948

FIRST PUBLISHED 1948

PRINTED IN GREAT BRITAIN
IN THE CITY OF OXFORD
AT THE ALDEN PRESS

CONTENTS

The chapters are numbered as in the Fifth Edition of Diels, *Fragmente der Vorsokratiker*. The numbers in brackets are those of the Fourth Edition.

viii

FOREWORD

THIS book is a complete translation of the fragments of the Pre-Socratic philosophers given in Diels, *Fragmente der Vorsokratiker*, Fifth Edition (B-sections).

Comments on readings and interpretation have been confined to footnotes, and are restricted to the minimum; for further discussion, the reader is referred to my *Companion to the Pre-Socratic Philosophers*, to which this book is ancillary.

The fragments have been translated in full except for the longer extracts from Gorgias, which are fully summarised. Summaries of contexts, and words inserted in explanation or for the sake of clarity, are given in italic type, in order to show the exact words of the writer when these are preserved. When no quotations survive, this has been stated for the sake of completeness, and an account derived from summaries in other ancient writers will be found in the *Companion*.

K. F.

ANCILLA TO
THE PRE-SOCRATIC PHILOSOPHERS

1. ORPHEUS

ORPHEUS lived probably in Thrace, in pre-Homeric times. Aristotle believed that he never existed; but to other ancient writers he was a real person, though living in remote antiquity.

Nothing is known of any ancient Orphic writings. It was believed that Orpheus taught, but left no writings, and that the epic poetry attributed to him was written in the sixth century by Onomacritus.

The Orphic literature current in the time of the Neo-Platonists (third century A.D.) is now thought to be a collection of writings of different periods and varying outlook, dating from the sixth century B.C. to the beginning of the Christian era.

A large number of titles survive.[1]

There are also a number of gold plates from tombs, and a few papyrus fragments, which give Orphic instruction to the dead.

1. (PLATO, *Philebus* 66C): In the sixth generation, cease the ordered arrangement of your song!

2. (PLATO, *Cratylus* 402B, C): Ocean, fair-flowing, first began marriage, he who married his full sister on the mother's side, Tethys.

3. (*ib.* 400B, C: *The Orphics explained the name 'sôma' for the body with reference to the verb 'sôzesthai', to keep safe or guard, the simile being that of a prison*).

4. (PLATO, *Republic* 363C: *Orphic doctrine on rewards and punishments in the next world, ascribed to 'Musaeus and his son': the just are given a life of feasting and everlasting drunkenness, and some say they shall leave children and grandchildren behind; the unjust are plunged into mud or made to carry water in sieves*).

5. (*ib.* 364E: *The Orphic books give instruction on purification, both private and communal, by means of sacrifice both for the living and the dead. These they call 'Teletai', 'rites of initiation', which if performed will save us from hurt in the next world, whereas if we fail to perform them, dire pains await us*).

5a. (PLATO, *Laws* 669D: *on incompatible elements in music. Poets who mixed up such elements in their compositions would*

---

[1] For list and discussion, see *Companion*, pp. 5-8.

I

provoke the laughter of all men who, as Orpheus says) have come to the time of enjoyment.

6. (*ib.* 715E: *as the ancient saying goes*) God holds the beginning and end, and the middle of all existing things.

6a. (*ib.* 829D: *Nobody is to sing a song not approved by the Guardians, not even if it be sweeter than the hymns of Thamyrus and Orpheus*).

7. (PLATO, *Symposium* 218B: *Alcibiades bids the uninitiated depart. Cp. the Orphic command*): Ye uninitiated, close the doors!

8. (PLATO, *Timaeus* 40D: *the 'descendants of the gods', as the Orphics[1] call themselves, give the following account of the origin of the other gods*): The children of Earth and Heaven were Ocean and Tethys, and from these came Phorcys, Cronos and Rhea, and their contemporaries; and from Cronos and Rhea came Zeus and Hera and all those whom we know, said to be their brothers and sisters, and others still, their offspring.

9. (ARISTOTLE, *Metaphysics* 1071b; 1091b: *The Theologoi generate all things from Night. The ancient poets agree that the Ruler is not Night and Heaven or Chaos or Ocean, but Zeus*).

10. (*ib.* 983B: *the ancient Theologoi made Ocean and Tethys the parents of Creation, and the oath of the gods in Water, or Styx as they called it*).

10a. (ARISTOTLE, *de gen. anim.* 734a: *The so-called epic poems of Orpheus say that the various organs — heart, lungs, liver, eyes, etc. — were formed successively: for he says therein that the animals come into being in the same way as a net is woven*).

11. (ARISTOTLE, *de anima,* 410b: *Discussion on whether all living things, including plants, have Soul: in the so-called Orphic poems, the poet says that Soul is borne along by the winds, and enters from the Whole when the creatures inhale*).

12. (DAMASCIUS: *The Theologia in Eudemus, attributed to Orpheus, says nothing about the Intelligible. He gave Night as the original Element. In the current Orphic Rhapsôdiae, the theology concerning the Intelligible is roughly as follows: for the One original Element, Time; for the Two, Aether and Chaos; and in the place*

---

[1] The Orphics are not named here, but are obviously meant.

2

of Being, the Egg; this triad come first. At the second stage comes either the Egg Fertilised, as God, or the Bright Robe, or the Cloud; from these comes Phanês. At the third stage come Mêtis as Intellect, Erikepaîos as Power, Phanês as Father.

ACHILLES: *The Orphics say that the Sphere is like an Egg, the vault of Heaven being the shell, and the Aether the skin).*

13. (DAMASCIUS: *The Orphic theogony given in Hieronymus and Hellanicus is not the same: it gives the first two elements as Water and Earth. The third Element was begotten of these two, and was a serpent having the heads of a bull and a lion with the face of a god in between; it had wings, and was called Ageless Time, or Unchanging Heracles. With him was united Necessity or Adrasteia, an element having no body, and spread over the whole universe, fastening it together. Time, the serpent, produced a three-fold offspring: Aether, Chaos and Erebus; in these, Time begat the Egg. At the third stage came a god without body, with golden wings, and bulls' heads on his flanks, and on his head a huge changing serpent. This theogony sings of Prôtogonos (First-born), and calls Zeus the Marshaller of All Things).*

(ATHENAGORAS: *Orpheus was the first theologian. He gave Water as the beginning of the Whole; from Water came Mud, and from both came a serpent, Heracles or Time. This Heracles produced a huge Egg, which split into two, forming Gê (Earth) and Ouranos (Heaven). Heaven united with Earth and produced the female Fates, and the male Giants and Cyclôpês. Ouranos flung the males into Tartarus, whereat Earth in anger produced the Titans):*

Lady Earth produced the sons of Ouranos, who are also called Titans,[1] because they have been punished by great starry Ouranos.

14. (PS.-DEMOSTHENES: *Implacable and reverend Justice, which Orpheus, who revealed to us the most holy rites, says is seated beside the throne of Zeus and looks upon all mortal happenings).*

15. (MARMOR PARIUM: *From the time when . . .[2] son published his poem, the Rape of Persephone and the search of Demeter and the gift of corn to men).*

(ORPHIC ARGONAUTICA: *The wandering of Demeter, her sorrow for Persephonê, and her lawgiving).*

---

[1] Τιτῆνες from τίνεσθαι.
[2] 'Orpheus, Oiagros' and Calliope's (*son*)' is supplied in the blank space here.

3

15a. *(Berlin Papyrus: paraphrase of an Orphic version of the Hymn to Demeter):*

Orpheus was the son of Oiagros and the Muse Calliopê; and the Lord of the Muses, Apollo, nodded towards him so that he became inspired and wrote his Hymns, which to a slight extent Musaeus corrected and wrote down, and he gave the sacred rites (orgies) of Orpheus to be revered by Greeks and barbarians, being deeply concerned with rites, purifications and oracles. The goddess Demeter . . . whom Orpheus gave as the sister of Zeus, others as the mother. There is no need to recall these things to the recollection of the pious.

(Homer's Hymn to Demeter, 418, 420-3 follow.)

(After the Rape of Persephone) Demeter mourns for her daughter. Calliopê and Cleisidicê and Dêmonassa having come with the queen to get water, inquire of Demeter as if she were a mortal — though Musaeus says in his poems that she joined them because of some need.

(Demeter nurses Dêmophon, infant son of the queen Baubô: she anoints him with oil and cradles him in the fire. Baubô sees this and screams. Demeter says):

'Foolish and wretched mortals, having foreknowledge neither of the evil nor of the good in prospect for you!'

(The baby is burnt up. The goddess reveals herself):

'I am Demeter, bringer of seasons, of bright gifts. What god of heaven, or who among mortal men, has seized Persephone and reft her dear soul?'

(The homecoming of Celeus, and story of Triptolemus)

Whence it (the poem) is called 'The Descent' (into Hades).

16. *(Apollonius Rhodius, 'Argonautica', I. 494: Orpheus, having lifted up his lyre, tried his song. He sang that Earth and Heaven and Sea formerly were fitted together into one form, and separated through destructive Hate; and that there are, as a perpetual sign in the Aether, the stars, the moon and the paths of the sun; and how the mountains rose, and how the singing rivers with their nymphs and all things that move were created. And he sang how first of all Ophiôn and Eurynomê daughter of Ocean held sway on snowy Olympus, and one was like Cronos in honour, with his power and might, and the other like Rhea; but they fell into the streams of Ocean. These then (Cronos and Rhea) for a while ruled over the Titans, blessed gods, while Zeus was still young, still*

4

thinking as a child, and was dwelling in the Dictaean cave, and the earth-born Cyclopes had not yet strengthened him with bolt, thunder and lightning, which give glory to Zeus.

Gold plates from tombs in Italy and Crete.[1]

17. *(From Petelia, fourth-third century* B.C.*)*
You will find a spring on the left of the halls of Hades, and beside it a white cypress growing. Do not even go near this spring. And you will find another, from the Lake of Memory, flowing forth with cold water. In front of it are guards. You must say, 'I am the child of Gê (Earth) and of starry Ouranos (Heaven); this you yourselves also know. I am dry with thirst and am perishing. Come, give me at once cold water flowing forth from the Lake of Memory.' And they themselves will give you to drink from the divine spring, and then thereafter you shall reign with the other heroes.

17a. *(From Eleuthernae (Crete), second century* B.C.*)*
A I am dry with thirst and am perishing.
B Come, drink, I pray, from the ever-flowing spring on the right, where the cypress is. Who are you, and whence?
A I am the son of Earth and starry Heaven.

18. *(From Thurii, fourth-third century* B.C.*)*
I come from the pure, O pure Queen of the earthly ones, Euclês, Eubouleus, and ye other immortal gods! I too claim to be of your blessed race, but Fate and other immortal gods conquered me, *(and sent)* the star-smiting thunder. And I flew out from the hard and deeply-grievous circle, and stepped on to the crown with my swift feet, and slipped into the bosom of the Mistress, the Queen of the Underworld. And I stepped out from the crown with my swift feet.
'Happy and blessed one, you shall be a god instead of a mortal.'
I have fallen as a kid into milk.

19. *(From Thurii: for a woman)*
I come pure from the pure, Queen of the Underworld, Euclês, Eubouleus and all other gods! For I too claim to be

[1] See Harrison, *Prolegomena*, Appendix by Gilbert Murray; Guthrie, *Orpheus and Greek Religion*, pp. 172-3; Freeman, *Companion to the Pre-Socratic Philosophers*, pp. 16-7.

of your race. And I have paid the penalty for unjust deeds, whether Fate conquered me ... with the thunderbolt and the lightning flash. Now a suppliant I come to noble Persephone, that she may be kind and send me to the seats of the pure.

19a. (*From Rome: for a woman*)
I come pure from the pure, Queen of the Underworld, Euclês, Eubouleus, noble child of Zeus! And I have this gift of Memory prized by men.
'Caecilia Secundina, come, made divine by the Law!'

20. (*From Thurii*)
But whenever a soul leaves the light of the sun — enter on the right where one must if one has kept all (*the laws*) well and truly. Rejoice at the experience! This you have never before experienced: you have become a god instead of a man. You have fallen as a kid into milk. Hail, hail, as you travel on the right, through the holy meadow and groves of Persephone!

21. (*From the same place*).
To Earth, first-born Mother, Cybelian Korê said: . . .
Of Demeter . . . All-seeing Zeus.
O Sun, Fire, you went through all towns, when you appeared with the Victories and Fortunes and all-wise Fate, where you increase the brightness of the festival with your lordship, O glorious deity! By you are all things subdued, all things over-powered, all things smitten! The decrees of Fate must every-where be endured. O Fire, lead me to the Mother, if the fast can endure, to fast for seven nights and days! For there was a seven-day fast, O Olympian Zeus and all-seeing Sun . . .

22. (CLEMENT of ALEXANDRIA: *Orphic terms from the poem On Orpheus by Epigenes*).
Shuttles with bent carriages (*ploughs*)
Warp-threads (*furrows*)
Thread (*seed*)
Tears of Zeus (*rain*)
Fates clothed in white (*phases of the moon*)
Little flower (*spring*)
Workless (*epithet of night*)
Gorgonian (*epithet of the moon, because of the face in it.*)
Aphrodite (*time for seed-sowing*)

6

23. (*Papyrus, third century* B.C.)
... in order that he may find
... on account of the rite they paid the penalty of their
fathers. Save me, Brimô, Demeter Rhea, and armed
Curêtês! ...
So that we may perform beautiful sacrifices ...
Goat and bull, limitless gifts ...
And by the law of the river...
Of the goat, and let him eat the rest of the flesh. Let no
uninitiated look on!
... dedicating to the ...
... prayer ...
I call on ... and Eubouleus, and call the (*Maenads*) who
cry Euoi ...
You having parched with thirst the friends of (*the feast*)...
... of Demeter and Pallas for us ...
King Irekepaigos, save me, (*Phanes*)!
(*The end is mutilated, but there is a reference to the toys of
Dionysus*): top, rattle, dice-bones, or mirror.

2. MUSAEUS

MUSAEUS, said to be of ATHENS, was thought to have lived in pre-Homeric
times.
He was regarded as a follower of Orpheus, and titles of poems were
attributed to him.

1. (SCHOLIAST on Apollonius Rhodius: *Musaeus in his
'Titanographia' says that Cadmus set forth from the Delphic shrine
led by the heifer*).

2. (*ib.*: *Medea sprinkled the drug with a juniper-branch, a tree
sacred to Apollo, and led the serpent by means of an incantation*).

3. (ARISTOTLE): The eagle lays three (*eggs*), hatches out two,
and neglects the third.

4. Art is ever far better than strength.

5. In the same way the life-giving earth sends up the
leaves: some it withers away on the ash-trees, others it sends
forth. So too the generation and race of mankind also circle
round.

6. (CLEMENT: *Eugamon of Cyrene appropriated the work of Musaeus 'On the Thesprotians', and published it as his own*).

7. (CLEMENT: *Hesiod in his 'Melampous' writes: 'It is sweet to learn all the things which the immortals have fixed for mortals as a clear sign of things unhappy and things good.' These lines are taken word for word from Musaeus*).

8. (Ps.-ERATOSTHENES: *Musaeus tells how Zeus at birth was handed over by Rhea to Themis, and by Themis to Amalthea, who gave him to the Goat, the daughter of the Sun, to rear in the caves of Crete. When he grew up and went to war with the Titans, he used the skin of the Goat as his shield because it was invulnerable and bore a Gorgon's face in the middle. He set the Goat in the sky as a constellation, while he himself acquired the epithet Aigiochos, 'goat-skin holder'*).

9. (*Melitê, a deme of the tribe Cecrôpis, was a daughter of Apollo according to Musaeus, not a daughter of Myrmex as Hesiod says*).

10. (*Triptolemus was the son of Ocean and Earth*).

11. (*From a poem 'Eumolpia', attributed to Musaeus*):
Forthwith the voice of Chthoniê uttered a wise word, and with her Pyrcôn, the servant of glorious Earth-Shaker.

12. (*The head of Zeus, when Athena was born, was split by Palamon, not by Hephaestus*).

13. (*Argos begat four Aethiopian kings by Celainô daughter of Atlas*).

14. (*In the theogony of Musaeus, Tartarus and Night came first*).

15. (*There were two generations of Muses*).

16. (*Zeus, after union with Asteria, gave her to Persês, son of a Titan; to him she bore Hecatê*).

17. (*Shooting stars are borne up from Ocean and generated in the Aether*).

18. (*The Hyades, nurses of Dionysus, are five in number; they are so-called because of their lamentation for their brother Hyas, killed while hunting. They are the daughters of Aethra and Ocean, and sisters of the seven Pleiades*).

8

19. (*The sea starwort, Tripolion: useful for everything, hence men pitch tents and dig it by night*).

19a. (*Hymns to Dionysus attributed to Orpheus and Musaeus. Orpheus composed them, Musaeus corrected them to a slight extent and copied them down*).

20. (*Musaeus wrote a 'Hymn to Demeter' for the Lycomidae; this told how Caucon son of Celaenos son of Phlyos took the rites of the Great Goddesses from Eleusis to Andania in Messenia in the reign of Polycaon and his wife Messênê*).

20a. (HERODOTUS, VII. 6: *Onomacritus an Athenian soothsayer was banished by Hipparchus for having inserted a line into the writings of Musaeus, namely that the islands off Lemnos would disappear under the sea*).

21. (HERODOTUS, VIII. 96: *Battle of Salamis: the west wind carried many of the wrecked ships on to the shore of Attica called Côlias; thus an oracle regarding this sea-battle by Musaeus and others was fulfilled*).

22. (*Oracle of Musaeus applied by the Athenians to the Battle of Aegospotami*):
On the Athenians is coming a severe storm through the baseness of their leaders, but there will be a consolation: they will completely bow the city down, but they will pay the penalty.

3. EPIMENIDES OF CRETE

EPIMENIDES of CRETE (Phaestos or Cnossus): date uncertain, but he probably lived in the late sixth and early fifth centuries B.C.

He was sometimes included in the list of the Seven Sages, in place of Periander. A number of epic poems were ascribed to him, giving an Orphic cosmogony; and a prose work on Cretan affairs, which was actually of later date, but was used by Diodorus.

1. (PAUL, *Epistle to Titus*, I. 12: *One of the Cretans, their own prophet, said of them*): The Cretans are always liars, evil beasts, lazy stomachs. (*Clement says that Paul means Epimenides, Jerome that it came from the Oracles of Epimenides*).

2. (*From his Epic poems*): I too am of the race of the fair-tressed moon, who with a dread shudder shook off the wild lion; and strangling him in Nemea because of revered Hera, (*the divine strength of Heracles overcame him*).

3. (ARISTOTLE, *Politics* 1252b: *Epimenides calls members of the same household*) sharers of the smoke.

4. (ARISTOTLE, *Rhetoric* 1418a; *Epimenides gave his oracles not about the future, but on things in the past which were obscure*).

5. (DAMASCIUS: *Epimenides gave the first elements as Air and Night, from which were created Tartarus, from which sprang two Titans; these having united produced the Egg, from which again another generation sprang*).

6. (PAUSANIAS: *Epimenides also makes Styx the daughter of Ocean, and unites her not with Pallas but with an unknown Peiras, to whom she bore Echidna*).

7. (*Epimenides says that the Harpies are the children of Ocean, and were slain near (Rhegium?)*).

8. (*The story of Typho: in Epimenides' version, Typho entered the palace while Zeus was asleep; and Zeus killed him with a thunderbolt*).

9. (*Epimenides agrees with certain others that the Harpies guard the apples, but says that they are the same as the Hesperides*).

10. (PLUTARCH: *Epimenides said of Munychia that*) the Athenians would eat it up with their own teeth, if they foresaw what harm it would do to the city.

11. (PLUTARCH: *Epimenides refuted the story that eagles or swans setting out from the ends of the earth met in the middle at Delphi, the so-called Omphalos*): There was no Omphalos, either in the centre of the earth or of the sea. If any there be, it is visible to the gods, not visible to mortals.

12. (*Epimenides adds a fifth to the sons of Phrixus, Presbôn by name*).

13. (*Aiêtês was a Corinthian, and his mother was Ephyra*).

14. (*Endymion in heaven fell in love with Hera, and Zeus condemned him to eternal sleep*).

15. (*Laius married Eurycleia daughter of Ecphas, and Oedipus was her son*).

16. (*The children of Zeus and Callistô were Pan and Arcas, twins*).

17. (*Epimenides and Hesiod agree on the names of the thirteen suitors slain by Oenomaus*).

18. (*Rhodes is the daughter of Ocean*).

19. (*The Eumenides are the daughters of Cronos*): From him were born fairhaired golden Aphrodite, the immortal Fates, and the Erinyes of changeful gifts.

20. (DIODORUS: '*I have followed the most trustworthy authorities on Cretan affairs, Epimenides the Theologian, Dosiades, Sosicrates and Laosthenes*').

21. (ARATUS: '*Holy Goat, of whom the story goes that she suckled Zeus, and the priest-interpreters of Zeus·call her Olenian*').

22. (ARATUS: *The story that Cynosoura and Helicê were placed in the heavens because they looked after Zeus in the Idaean cave, when the Dictaean Kourêtês hid him from Cronos*).

23. (*Cretan story that Zeus when hiding from Cronos changèd himself and his nurses into a serpent and bears respectively, and after he had taken over the kingship, placed these forms in the Arctic Circle*).

24. (*The story of Aigokerôs: honoured because he was a foster-brother of Zeus, being with him in Crete when he fought the Titans. Aigokerôs is believed to have discovered the horn, the sound of which put the Titans to flight. He and his mother the Goat were placed in the heavens by Zeus: because he found the horn in the sea, Aigokerôs has a fish-tail*).

25. (*The Crown was a gift of Dionysus to Ariadnê; later he placed it in the heavens*).

Late forgery, drawn from Neo-Pythagoreanism.
26. (*The Dioscuri were male and female, one called Time, as being a Monad, the other called Nature, as being a Dyad; for from the Monad and the Dyad, all numbers which produce life and soul have sprung*).

4. HÊSIOD OF ASCRA

Hêsiod of Ascra flourished probably in the eighth century B.C.

Apart from his *Theogony* and *Works and Days*, another poem called *Astrologia* or *Astronomia* was sometimes attributed to him by ancient authors. This poem was probably written in the sixth century B.C.

1. Mortals call them the Pleiads.

2. The stormy Pleiads are setting.

3. Then vanish the Pleiads.

4. (*The morning setting of the Pleiads coincides with the autumnal equinox, according to Epimenides*).

5. *The Hyades:* They are Nymphs like the Graces: Phaesylê and Corônis and fair-garlanded Cleeia, lovely Phaeô and Eudôrê of the long robe, whom the tribes of men on earth call Hyades.

6. (*The Great Bear: a daughter of Lycaon in Arcadia chose the life of a huntress with Artemis on the mountains. Being seduced by Zeus, she continued, undetected by the goddess, until the latter discovered her pregnancy on seeing her bathing, and changed her into a bear. She bore the so-called Arcas. When on the mountain she was hunted by goatherds and handed over to Lycaon with her baby. Later she was believed to have set foot in the sacred precinct of Zeus in ignorance of the law; being pursued by her own son and about to be killed, she was saved by Zeus and placed among the stars.*

    (*Boôtês: he is said to be Arcas son of Zeus and Callistô. When Zeus had seduced her, Lycaon served him with a dish of the infant's flesh.*

    (*Callistô was one of the Nymphs*).

7. (*Ôrion: son of Minô and Poseidon, was granted by his father the power of walking on the waves. While in Chios he seduced Meropê, and was blinded and expelled by her father Oenopiôn. He went to Lemnos, where Hephaestus in pity gave him a guide, Cêdalion; carrying him on his shoulders, Orion went eastwards until his blindness was cured by the sun. He then returned to seek vengeance on Oenopiôn, but the latter was hidden underground by his people. Baulked in his search, Orion went to Crete and gave himself up to hunting, with Artemis and Leto. He threatened to*

kill all the animals on earth, but Gê in anger sent a huge serpent whose sting killed him. Zeus at the request of Artemis and Leto placed him among the stars for his valour).

8. (*Straits of Messina: Orion, after the sea had opened up, piled up the headland of Pelôris on the Sicilian side and made the precinct of Poseidon, which was particularly revered by the inhabitants. Orion then crossed to Euboea and settled there).*

5. PHÔCUS OF SAMOS

PHÔCUS of SAMOS: date unknown.

He was credited with a verse work on *Nautical Astronomy* sometimes ascribed to Thales. Nothing is known of its contents.

6. CLEOSTRATUS OF TENEDOS

CLEOSTRATUS of TENEDOS lived in the sixth century B.C.

He wrote an astronomical work called *Astrologia* or *Phaenomena.*

1. (SCHOLIAST on Euripides, *Rhesus* 528: *explanation of the words 'first signs'.*): But when for the third day over the eighty (*Arctophylax*) remains (*shining, then the 'first signs'*) of the Scorpion fall into the sea.[1]

2. (*He then, it is said, observed the signs in the Zodiac, beginning with the Ram and the Archer).*

3. (*He is said to have been the first to point out the Kids among the constellations).*

4. (*The eight-year cycle is commonly attributed to Eudoxus of Cnidus, but they say that it was Cleostratus of Tenedos who first devised it).*

7. PHERECŶDES OF SYROS

PHERECŶDES of SYROS: date uncertain; he may have lived in the seventh century, or middle of the sixth century B.C.

He was said to have been the first to write in prose. His book, extant in antiquity, was called *Heptamychos* (Seven-Chambered Cosmos) or *Theocrasia* (Divine Mingling) or *Theogonia.*

[1] Restoration and meaning uncertain; for discussion, see *Companion*, p. 34, note 3.

1.   Zas (*Zeus*) and Time existed always, and Chthoniê; but Chthoniê acquired the name Gê, since Zas gives earth to her as a gift of honour.

1a.   (*Pherecydes, like Thales, gives water as the first cause; he calls it Chaos, probably borrowing the term from Hesiod*).

2.   For him (*Zas*) they make the houses many and great. And when they had finished providing all this, and also furnishings and men-servants and maid-servants and all else required, when all is ready, they carry out the wedding. On the third day of the wedding, Zas makes a robe, large and fair, and on it he embroiders Earth and Ōgenos (*Ocean*) and his dwelling . . . 'For wishing your marriage to take place, I honour you with this. Therefore receive my greeting and be my wife.' This they say was the first unveiling ceremony, and hence arose the custom among gods and men. And she answers him, receiving the robe from him . . .

3.   (*Zeus when about to create changed into Eros, because by combining the Cosmos out of opposites he brought it into harmony and love, and sowed likeness in all, and unity extending through all things*).

4.   (*Story of the war between the two armies under Cronos (Saturn) and Ophioneus: after challenges and combats, a pact was made, that whichever side fell into Ocean should have lost, and the other side should be victors and rule the heavens. To this can be traced the Mysteries concerning Titans and Giants who are said to have made war on the gods, and also the Egyptian stories of Typho, Horus and Osiris*).

5.   (*Comment by Pherecydes on* Homer; *Iliad*, 1. 590 *and* xv. 18): Below this part of the world is the Tartarean part; its guardians are the daughters of Boreas, the Harpies and the Storm-wind. Thither does Zeus banish any god who commits an act of lawlessness.

6.   Hollows, ditches, caves and gates.

7.   Outflow.

8.   (*Aethalides had from Hermes the gift of transmigration of his soul from Hades and earth and vice versa*).

9. Rhê (*Rhea*).

10. (*Forms for possessive pronoun 'mine'*).

11. (*Forms for personal pronouns 'we, you, they'*).

12. (*Word used by the gods for 'table'*).

13. (*Pherecydes does not agree that Zeus and Hera are the father and mother of the gods*).

13a. (*Ambrosia the food of the gods*).

Spurious.

14. (*The pupils of Pherecydes called the Dyad Boldness and Impulse and Opinion, because the true and false are in Opinion*).

8. THEAGENES OF RHÊGIUM

THEAGENES of RHÊGIUM lived in the time of Cambyses (529-522 B.C.).
     He was the first scholar known to have applied the allegorical method of interpretation to Homer. No writings survive.

9. ACUSILÃUS OF ARGOS

ACUSILÃUS of ARGOS lived probably in the sixth century B.C.
     He wrote a prose work on the origins of Gods and men, called *Genealogies*.

1. (*Chaos was the first principle, and after it the pair, Erebus the male and Night the female; from their union sprang Aether, Eros and Mêtis; and the other gods are derived from these*).

2. (PLATO, *Symposium* 178B: *Acusilaus agrees with Hesiod that Chaos came first, and after Chaos Earth and Eros*).

3. (*Eros the son of Night and Aether*).

4. (*Koios: among names of male and female Titans*).

5. (*Iris is the messenger of all the gods. The Harpies guard the apples of the Hesperides*).

6. (*Cerberus is the son of Echidnê and Typho; also other monsters, including the eagle that eats the liver of Prometheus*).

7. (*Typho attacked the kingdom of Zeus*).

8. (*Phorcys was the son of Eidothea and father of the Graeae. Proteus and Tithonus, though old, were immortal. There are two generations of goddesses: the older married, and the younger unmarried, like Artemis and Athene, Peace and Justice*).

9. (*Asclepius was killed by Zeus*).

9a. (*Ouranos flung the Hundred-armed Giants into Tartarus, fearing that they would prevail, and knowing their sins*).

9b. (*Acusilaus like Homer briefly tells the story of the giants*).

9c. (*Heracles died in the fire*).

10. (*Apollo was about to be flung into Tartarus by Zeus, but on the supplication of Leto he was allowed to serve a man, Admetus, instead*).

11. (*Pelasgus, son of Niobe and Zeus, gave his name to the Pelasgians of the Peloponnese*).

12. (*Io the daughter of Peirên*).

13. (*Argus was earthborn*).

14. (*The daughters of Proetus were driven mad because they had disparaged the wooden statue of Hera*).

15. (*The Cretan bull, capture of which formed the seventh labour of Heracles, was the bull that ferried Europa across the sea*).

16. (*Actaeon, eaten on Cithaeron by his own dogs, was punished by madness for having wooed Semele*).

17. (*Menelaus had a son Megapenthês by Têrêis*).

18. (*The river Asôpus is the son of Pêrô and Poseidon*).

19. (*Zêtês and Calais were destroyed by Heracles near Tenos*).

20. (*Phorôneus was the first man. When he was king in Argos, the Great Flood occurred in Attica*).

21. (*Achelôos is the oldest of the rivers*): Ocean marries Tethys his own sister; from them spring three thousand rivers, but Achelôos is the oldest and most honoured.

22. (*The Homeridae are a clan in Chios*).

23. (*The men of old lived for a thousand years*).

24. (*Mycênae was named after Mycêneus son of Spartôn, who was a son of Phorôneus*).

25. (*The sons of Phrixus had as their mother Iophôssê daughter of Aeêtês*).

26. (*Story of Endymion*).

27. (*Scylla daughter of Phorcys and Hecatê*).

28. (*The Phaeacians sprang from blood that dripped from Ouranos to earth on his castration*).

29. (*The Fleece was not golden, but dyed purple by the sea*).

30. (*There are three winds, Borras, Zephyr, Notos; the epithet 'bright' applies only to Zephyr*).

31. (*Version of the Trojan War: Aphrodite, hearing an oracle that the throne of Priam would fall and the descendants of Anchises would rule Troy, united with Anchises in his old age and bore Aeneas; wishing to bring about the downfall of the house of Priam she inspired Paris with a passion for Helen; and after the abduction she pretended to be fighting on the Trojan side, whereas she was glossing over their defeat, in order that they should not fall into despair and hand over Helen*).

32. (*Anchises son of Cleonymus, Echepôlus son of Anchises*).

33. (*The mother of Deucalion was Hêsionê daughter of Ocean, and his father was Prometheus*).

34. (*Eurypylus was the son of Astyochê and Têlephus. Priam bribed Astyochê with a golden vine to allow her son to go to the war*).

35. (*Ôreithyia, daughter of Erechtheus, was carried away by Boreas as she walked in the procession to Athene Polias. Boreas took her to Thrace, where she bore Zêtês and Calais, who sailed with the Argonauts*).

36. (*Ithaca and its mountain Nêriton were named after Ithacus and Nêritus, descendants of Zeus, who settled first in Cephallenia and then on Ithaca*).

37. (*All creatures that sting come from the blood of Typho*).

38. (*Deucalion and Pyrrha made men by throwing stones behind them*).

39. (*Corônis preferred Ischys to Apollo, because she feared to be despised by a god and wished to marry a mortal*).

40. (*From Cabîrô and Hephaestus sprang Camillus, from him the three Cabîri, ... three Nymphs, the Cabiridae*).

40a. Poseidon united with Caenê daughter of Elatus. Afterwards, since she did not wish to have a child by him or anyone else, Poseidon turned her into a man (Caeneus) invulnerable, having strength greater than that of all the men of his day; and whenever anyone tried to wound him with iron or bronze, he was at once held fast. This Caeneus became king of the Lapithae and used to make war on the Centaurs. Later he set up a javelin in the market-place, and demanded to be accounted a god. This was displeasing to the gods, and Zeus seeing him doing this threatened him and sent the Centaurs against him, and they cut him down to the ground where he stood, and set a rock above as a grave-stone, and he died.

Doubtful

41. (SCHOLIAST on Pindar, *Olympian*, VII. 42: *Pindar appears to have used the ancient historiographer in his genealogy of Amyntor*).

10. THE SEVEN SAGES

THE SEVEN SAGES lived in the latter half of the seventh, and the early sixth, centuries B.C.

The list of the Sages varies. Only four were universally agreed upon: Thales, Bias, Pittacus, Solon. The earliest list, which adds Cleobulus, Myson, Chilon, is given by Plato in the *Protagoras*.

They represented the practical wisdom of Greece. Many sayings were attributed to them, of which the best-known are: 'Know thyself', and 'Nothing too much'; these they dedicated to Apollo at Delphi.

11. THALES OF MILÊTUS

THALES of MILÊTUS was in his prime about 585 B.C.

Whether he ever wrote a book is unknown; if he did, no genuine fragment survives.

1. (*Title: 'Nautical Astronomy'*).

2. (*There are two Hyades, one north and one south*).

18

3. The much-discussed four substances — of which we say the chief is Water, making it as it were the one Element — by combination and solidification and coagulation of the substances in the universe mingle with one another. In what way, I have already explained in Book One.

4. (*Titles: 'On the Solstice'. 'On the Equinox'*).

12. ANAXIMANDER OF MILÊTUS

ANAXIMANDER of MILÊTUS was in his prime about 560 B.C.
The title or titles of any works of his are unknown.

1. The Non-Limited is the original material of existing things; further, the source from which existing things derive their existence is also that to which they return at their destruction, according to necessity; for they give justice and make reparation to one another for their injustice, according to the arrangement of Time.

2. This (essential nature, whatever it is, of the Non-Limited) is everlasting and ageless.

3. (*The Non-Limited*) is immortal and indestructible.

4. Nozzle of the bellows.

5. (*The Earth is like*) a stone column.

13. ANAXIMENES OF MILÊTUS

ANAXIMENES of MILÊTUS was in his prime about 546 B.C.
He wrote one book, in 'simple and unextravagant Ionic'. One whole sentence only has survived.

1. (*Paraphrase containing the word*) Loose. (=*rare*).

2. As our soul, being air, holds us together, so do breath and air surround the whole universe.

2a. (*The sun is broad*) like a leaf.

(*Spurious*)
3. Air is near to the incorporeal; and since we come into being by an efflux from this (*air*), it is bound to be both non-limited and rich so that it never fails.

14. PYTHAGORAS OF SAMOS

PYTHAGORAS of SAMOS was in his prime about 530 B.C.
He left no written works.

15-20. OLDER PYTHAGOREANS

OLDER PYTHAGOREANS: CERCÔPS, PETRÔN, BRO(N)TÎNUS, HIPPASOS,
CALLIPHÔN and DÊMOCÊDÊS, PARM(EN)ISCUS.
Nothing certain is known of any written works.

21. XENOPHANES OF COLOPHÔN

XENOPHANES of COLOPHÔN was in his prime about 530 B.C.
He wrote poems for recitation, in hexameters and elegiacs.

Elegiacs

1. For now, behold, the floor is clean, and so too the hands
of all, and the cups. One (*attendant*) places woven garlands
round our heads, another proffers sweet-scented myrrh in a
saucer. The mixing-bowl stands there full of good cheer, and
another wine is ready in the jar, a wine that promises never to
betray us, honeyed, smelling of flowers. In our midst the
frankincense gives forth its sacred perfume; and there is cold
water, sweet and pure. Golden loaves lie to hand, and the
lordly table is laden with cheese and with honey. The altar
in the centre is decked with flowers all over, and song and
revelry fill the mansion.

It is proper for men who are enjoying themselves first of all
to praise God with decent stories and pure words. But when
they have poured a libation and prayed for the power to do
what is just — for thus to pray is our foremost need — it is no
outrage to drink as much as will enable you to reach home
without a guide, unless you are very old. But the man whom
one must praise is he who after drinking expresses thoughts
that are noble, as well as his memory (*and his endeavour*)[1] concerning virtue allows, not treating of the battles of the Titans
or of the Giants, figments of our predecessors, nor of violent
civil war, in which tales there is nothing useful; but always to
have respect for the gods, *that* is good.

---

[1] τόνος (Diels), an unlikely emendation.

2. But if anyone were to win a victory with fleetness of foot, or fighting in the Pentathlon, where the precinct of Zeus lies between the springs of Pisa at Olympia, or in wrestling, or in virtue of the painful science of boxing, or in a dread kind of contest called Pancration: to the citizens he would be more glorious to look upon, and he would acquire a conspicuous seat of honour at competitions, and his maintenance would be provided out of the public stores by the City-State, as well as a gift for him to lay aside as treasure.

So too if he won a prize with his horses, he would obtain all these rewards, though not deserving of them as *I* am; for my craft (wisdom) is better than the strength of men or of horses. Yet opinion is altogether confused in this matter, and it is not right to prefer physical strength to noble Wisdom. For it is not the presence of a good boxer in the community, nor of one good at the Pentathlon or at wrestling, nor even of one who excels in fleetness of foot — which is highest in honour of all the feats of strength seen in men's athletic contests — it is not these that will give a City-State a better constitution. Small would be the enjoyment that a City-State would reap over the athletic victory of a citizen beside the banks of Pisa! These things do not enrich the treasure-chambers of the State.

3. (*The men of Colophon*), having learnt useless forms of luxury from the Lydians, as long as they were free from hateful tyranny, used to go to the place of assembly wearing all-purple robes, not less than a thousand of them in all: haughty, adorned with well-dressed hair, steeped in the scent of skilfully-prepared unguents.

4. (*The Lydians first struck coinage*).

5. Nor would anyone first pour the wine into the cup when mixing it, but rather the water, and on to that the pure wine.

6. For, having sent a kid's ham, you received in return the fat leg of a bull, a precious prize for a man whose fame shall reach all over Hellas, and shall not cease so long as the race of Hellenic bards exists.

7. Now again I shall pass to another theme, and shall show the way. . . .

. . . And once, they say, passing by when a puppy was being

beaten, he pitied it, and spoke as follows: 'Stop! Cease your beating, because this is really the soul of a man who was my friend: I recognised it as I heard it cry aloud.'

8. By now, seven-and-sixty years have been tossing my care-filled heart over the land of Hellas. From my birth till then (*that is, till his exile*), there were twenty-five years to be added to these, if indeed I am able to tell correctly of these matters.

9. Much feebler than an aged man.

Hexameters

10. Since from the beginning all have learnt in accordance with Homer . . .

11. Both Homer and Hesiod have attributed to the gods all things that are shameful and a reproach among mankind: theft, adultery, and mutual deception.

12. They have narrated every possible wicked story of the gods: theft, adultery, and mutual deception.

13. (*Homer was earlier than Hesiod*).

14. But mortals believe the gods to be created by birth, and to have their own (*mortals'*) raiment, voice and body.

15. But if oxen (and horses) and lions had hands or could draw with hands and create works of art like those made by men, horses would draw pictures of gods like horses, and oxen of gods like oxen, and they would make the bodies (of their gods) in accordance with the form that each species itself possesses.

16. Aethiopians have gods with snub noses and black hair, Thracians have gods with grey eyes and red hair.

17. (*The Bacchic branches*) of fir-wood stand round the firm-built dwelling.

18. Truly the gods have not revealed to mortals all things from the beginning; but mortals by long seeking discover what is better.

19. (*Xenophanes admired Thales for having predicted solar eclipses*).

22

20.   (*Xenophanes said that he had heard that Epimenidés lived to the age of* 154).

21.   (*Of Simonides*). Skinflint.

21a. Erykos (*Eryx, in Sicily*).

22.   One should hold such converse by the fire-side in the winter season, lying on a soft couch, well-fed, drinking sweet wine, nibbling peas: 'Who are you among men, and where from? How old are you, my good friend? What age were you when the Mede came?'

23.   There is one god, among gods and men the greatest, not at all like mortals in body or in mind.

24.   He sees as a whole, thinks as a whole, and hears as a whole.

25.   But without toil he sets everything in motion, by the thought of his mind.

26.   And he always remains in the same place, not moving at all, nor is it fitting for him to change his position at different times.

27.   For everything comes from earth and everything goes back to earth at last.

28.   This is the upper limit of the earth that we see at our feet, in contact with the air; but the part beneath goes down to infinity.

29.   All things that come into being and grow are earth and water.

30.   The sea is the source of water, and the source of wind. For neither could (the force of the wind blowing outwards from within come into being) without the great main (sea), nor the streams of rivers, nor the showery water of the sky; but the mighty main is the begetter of clouds and winds and rivers.

31.   The sun rushing on its way above the earth and giving it warmth.

32.   And she whom they call Iris, she too is actually a cloud, purple and flame-red and yellow to behold.

33. We all have our origin from earth and water.

34. And as for certain truth, no man has seen it, nor will there ever be a man who knows about the gods and about all the things I mention. For if he succeeds to the full in saying what is completely true, he himself is nevertheless unaware of it; and Opinion (seeming) is fixed by fate upon all things.

35. Let these things be stated as conjectural only, similar to the reality.

36. All appearances which exist for mortals to look at. . . .

37. Also, in (certain) caves, water drips down.

38. If God had not created yellow honey, they would say that figs were far sweeter.

39. Cherry-tree.

40. (Ionian dialect-word for a frog).

41. (Word for) A pit.

22. HÊRACLEITUS OF EPHESUS

HÊRACLEITUS of EPHESUS was in his prime about 500 B.C.

He wrote one book, covering all knowledge, metaphysical, scientific and political, in an oracular style.

1. The Law[1] (of the universe) is as here explained; but men are always incapable of understanding it, both before they hear it, and when they have heard it for the first time. For though all things come into being in accordance with this Law, men seem as if they had never met with it, when they meet with words (theories) and actions (processes) such as I expound, separating each thing according to its nature and explaining how it is made. As for the rest of mankind, they are unaware of what they are doing after they wake, just as they forget what they did while asleep.

2. Therefore one must follow (the universal Law, namely) that which is common (to all). But although the Law is

[1] Logos, the intelligible Law of the universe, and its reasoned statement by Heracleitus. See Companion, pp. 115 sqq.

universal, the majority live as if they had understanding peculiar to themselves.

3. (*On the size of the sun*): the breadth of a man's foot.

4. If happiness lay in bodily pleasures, we would call oxen happy when they find vetch to eat.

5. They purify themselves by staining[1] themselves with other blood, as if one were to step into mud in order to wash off mud. But a man would be thought mad[1] if any of his fellow-men should perceive him acting thus. Moreover, they talk to these statues (*of theirs*) as if one were to hold conversation with houses, in his ignorance of the nature of both gods and heroes.

6. The sun is new each day.

7. If all existing things turned to smoke, the nose would be the discriminating organ.

8. That which is in opposition is in concert, and from things that differ comes the most beautiful harmony.

9. Donkeys prefer chaff to gold.

10. Joints: whole and not whole, connected-separate, consonant-dissonant.

11. Every creature is driven to pasture with a blow.

12. Anhalation (*vaporisation*). Those who step into the same river have different waters flowing ever upon them. (Souls also are vaporised from what is wet).

13. Do not revel in mud. (*Swine enjoy mud rather than pure water*).

14. Night-ramblers, magicians, Bacchants, Maenads, Mystics: the rites accepted by mankind in the Mysteries are an unholy performance.

15. If it were not in honour of Dionysus that they conducted the procession and sang the hymn to the male organ (*the phallic hymn*), their activity would be completely shameless. But Hades is the same as Dionysus, in whose honour they rave and perform the Bacchic revels.

---

[1] Pun on μιαινόμενοι and μαίνεσθαι, which cannot be reproduced in English.

16. How could anyone hide from that which never sets?

17. For many men — those who encounter such things — do not understand them, and do not grasp them after they have learnt; but to themselves they seem (*to understand*).

18. If one does not hope, one will not find the unhoped-for, since there is no trail leading to it and no path.

19. Men who do not know how to listen or how to speak.

20. When they are born, they are willing to live and accept their fate (*death*); and they leave behind children to become victims of fate.

21. All that we see when we have wakened is death; all that we see while slumbering is sleep.

22. Those who seek gold dig much earth and find little.

23. They would not know the name of Right, if these things (*i.e. the opposite*) did not exist.

24. Gods and men honour those slain in war.

25. The greater the fate (*death*), the greater the reward.

26. In the night, a man kindles[1] a light because his sight is quenched; while living, he approximates to[1] a dead man during sleep; while awake, he approximates to one who sleeps.

27. There await men after they are dead things which they do not expect or imagine.

28. The most wise-seeming man knows, (*that is*), preserves, only what seems; furthermore, retribution will seize the fabricators of lies and the (*false*) witnesses.

29. The best men choose one thing rather than all else: everlasting fame among mortal men.[2] The majority are satisfied, like well-fed cattle.

30. This ordered universe (*cosmos*), which is the same for all, was not created by any one of the gods or of mankind, but it was ever and is and shall be ever-living Fire, kindled in measure and quenched in measure.

[1] Pun on ἅπτεται, 'kindles', and 'touches upon' (approximates to).
[2] Or: 'rather than things mortal'.

31. The changes of fire: first, sea; and of sea, half is earth and half fiery water-spout ... Earth[1] is liquified into sea, and retains its measure according to the same Law as existed before it became earth.

32. That which alone is wise is one; it is willing and unwilling to be called by the name of Zeus.

33. To obey the will of one man is also Law (*political law, Nomos*).

34. Not understanding, although they have heard, they are like the deaf. The proverb bears witness to them: 'Present yet absent.'

35. Men who love wisdom must be inquirers into very many things indeed.

36. To souls, it is death to become water; to water, it is death to become earth. From earth comes water, and from water, soul.

37. Pigs wash themselves in mud, birds in dust or ashes.

38. (*Thales was the first to study astronomy*).

39. In Priênê was born Bias son of Teutamos, whose fame (*or*, 'worth') is greater than that of the rest.

40. Much learning does not teach one to have intelligence; for it would have taught Hesiod and Pythagoras, and again, Xenophanes and Hecataeus.

41. That which is wise is one: to understand the purpose which steers all things through all things.

42. Homer deserves to be flung out of the contests and given a beating; and also Archilochus.

43. One should quench arrogance rather than a conflagration.

44. The people should fight for the Law (*Nomos*) as if for their city-wall.

45. You could not in your going find the ends of the soul, though you travelled the whole way: so deep is its Law (*Logos*).

[1] γῆ supplied by Kranz; otherwise, 'the sea is distributed'.

46.   Conceit: the sacred disease (*i.e. epilepsy*).

47.   Let us not conjecture at random about the greatest things.

48.   The bow is called Life,[1] but its work is death.

49.   One man to me is (*worth*) ten thousand, if he is the best.

49a.   In the same river, we both step and do not step, we are and we are not.

50.   When you have listened, not to me but to the Law (*Logos*), it is wise to agree that all things are one.

51.   They do not understand how that which differs with itself is in agreement: harmony consists of opposing tension, like that of the bow and the lyre.

52.   Time is a child playing a game of draughts; the kingship is in the hands of a child.

53.   War is both king of all and father of all, and it has revealed some as gods, others as men; some it has made slaves, others free.

54.   The hidden harmony is stronger (*or*, 'better') than the visible.

55.   Those things of which there is sight, hearing, knowledge: these are what I honour most.

56.   Men are deceived over the recognition of visible things, in the same way as Homer, who was the wisest of all the Hellenes; for he too was deceived by boys killing lice, who said: 'What we saw and grasped, that we leave behind; but what we did not see and did not grasp, that we bring.'

57.   Hesiod is the teacher of very many, he who did not understand day and night: for they are one.

58.   For instance, physicians, who cut and burn, demand payment of a fee, though undeserving, since they produce the same (*pains as the disease*).

59.   For the fuller's screw, the way, straight and crooked, is one and the same.

---

[1] Pun on βίος, Life, and βιός, bow.

60. The way up and down is one and the same.

61. Sea water is the purest and most polluted: for fish, it is drinkable and life-giving; for men, not drinkable and destructive.

62. . Immortals are mortal, mortals are immortal: (*each*) lives the death of the other, and dies their life.

63. When he (*God?*) is there, they (*the souls in Hades*) arise and become watchful guardians of the living and the dead.

64. The thunder-bolt (*i.e. Fire*) steers the universe.

65. Need and satiety.

66. Fire, having come upon them, will judge and seize upon (condemn) all things.

67. God is day-night, winter-summer, war-peace, satiety-famine. But he changes like (fire) which when it mingles with the smoke of incense, is named according to each man's pleasure.

68. (*Heracleitus called the shameful rites of the Mysteries*) Remedies.

69. (*There are two sorts of sacrifice: one kind offered by men entirely purified, as sometimes occurs, though rarely, in an individual, or a few easy to number; the other kind material*).[1]

70. Children's toys (*i.e. men's conjectures*).

71. (*One must remember also*) the man who forgets which way the road leads.

72. The Law (*Logos*): though men associate with it most closely, yet they are separated from it, and those things which they encounter daily seem to them strange.

73. We must not act and speak like men asleep.

74. (*We must not act like*) children of our parents.

75. Those who sleep are workers and share in the activities going on in the universe.

[1] Paraphrase in Iamblichus.

76. Fire lives the death of earth, and air lives the death of fire; water lives the death of air, earth that of water.

77. It is delight, or rather death, to souls to become wet... We live their (*the souls'*) death, and they (*the souls*) live our death.

78. Human nature has no power of understanding; but the divine nature has it.

79. Man is called childish compared with divinity, just as a boy compared with a man.

80. One should know that war is general (*universal*) and jurisdiction is strife, and everything comes about by way of strife and necessity.

81. (*On Pythagoras*). Original chief of wranglers.

82. (*The most handsome ape is ugly compared with the human race*).[1]

83. (*The wisest man will appear an ape in relation to God, both in wisdom and beauty and everything else*).[1]

84a. It rests from change. (*Elemental Fire in the human body*).

84b. It is a weariness to the same (*elements forming the human body*) to toil and to obey.

85. It is hard to fight against impulse; whatever it wishes, it buys at the expense of the soul.

86. (*Most of what is divine*) escapes recognition through unbelief.

87. A foolish man is apt to be in a flutter at every word (*or, 'theory': Logos*).

88. And what is in us is the same thing: living and dead, awake and sleeping, as well as young and old; for the latter (*of each pair of opposites*) having changed becomes the former, and this again having changed becomes the latter.

89. To those who are awake, there is one ordered universe common (*to all*), whereas in sleep each man turns away (*from this world*) to one of his own.

---

[1] Paraphrases in Plato, *Hippias Maior*.

90. There is an exchange: all things for Fire and Fire for all things, like goods for gold and gold for goods.

91. It is not possible to step twice into the same river. (*It is impossible to touch the same mortal substance twice, but through the rapidity of change*) they scatter and again combine (*or rather, not even 'again' or 'later', but the combination and separation are simultaneous*) and approach and separate.[1]

92. The Sibyl with raving mouth uttering her unlaughing, unadorned, unincensed words reaches out over a thousand years with her voice, through the (*inspiration of the*) god.

93. The lord whose oracle is that at Delphi neither speaks nor conceals, but indicates.

94. The sun will not transgress his measures; otherwise the Furies, ministers of Justice, will find him out.

95. It is better to hide ignorance (*though this is hard in relaxation and over wine*).

96. Corpses are more worthy to be thrown out than dung.

97. Dogs bark at those whom they do not recognise.

98. Souls have the sense of smell in Hades.

99. If there were no sun, so far as depended on the other stars it would be night.

100. (*The sun is in charge of the seasonal changes, and*) the Hours (Seasons) that bring all things.

101. I searched into myself.

101a. The eyes are more exact witnesses than the ears.

102. To God, all things are beautiful, good and just; but men have assumed some things to be unjust, others just.

103. Beginning and end are general in the circumference of the circle.

104. What intelligence or understanding have they? They believe the people's bards, and use as their teacher the populace, not knowing that 'the majority are bad, and the good are few'.[2]

---

[1] Phrases of Heracleitus quoted in Aristotle, *Metaphysics*.
[2] Saying attributed to Bias of Priênê. Diels, *Vors.*, ch. 10, 3, s. 1.

31

105.   Homer was an astrologer.

106.   (*Heracleitus reproached Hesiod for regarding some days as bad and others as good*). Hesiod was unaware that the nature of every day is one.

107.   The eyes and ears are bad witnesses for men if they have barbarian souls.

108.   Of all those whose discourse I have heard, none arrives at the realisation that that which is wise is set apart from all things.

109.   *See 95.*

110.   It is not better for men to obtain all that they wish.

111.   Disease makes health pleasant and good, hunger satisfaction, weariness rest.

112.   Moderation is the greatest virtue, and wisdom is to speak the truth and to act according to nature, paying heed (*thereto*).

113.· The thinking faculty is common to all.

114.   If we speak with intelligence,[1] we must base our strength on that which is common to all,[1] as the city on the Law (*Nomos*), and even more strongly. For all human laws are nourished by one, which is divine. For it governs as far as it will, and is sufficient for all, and more than enough.

115.   The soul has its own Law (*Logos*), which increases itself (*i.e. grows according to its needs*).

116.   All men have the capacity of knowing themselves and acting with moderation.

117.   A man, when he gets drunk, is led stumbling along by an immature boy, not knowing where he is going, having his soul wet.

118.   A dry (desiccated) soul is the wisest and best.

119.   Character for man is destiny.

120.   The limits of morning and evening are the Bear and,

---

[1] Pun on ξὺν νῷ and ξυνῷ.

opposite the Bear, the boundary-mark of Zeus god of the clear sky.

121.   The Ephesians would do well to hang themselves, every adult man, and bequeath their City-State to adolescents, since they have expelled Hermodôrus, the most valuable man among them, saying: 'Let us not have even one valuable man; but if we do, let him go elsewhere and live among others.'

122.   (*Word for*) Approximation.

123.   Nature likes to hide.

124.   The fairest universe is but a dust-heap piled up at random.

125.   The 'mixed drink' (*Kykeôn: mixture of wine, grated cheese and barley-meal*) also separates if it is not stirred.

125a.   May wealth not fail you, men of Ephesus, so that you may be convicted of your wickedness!

126.   Cold things grow hot, hot things grow cold, the wet dries, the parched is moistened.

Doubtful and spurious fragments[1]
126a.   According to the law of the seasons, the number Seven is combined in the moon, separated in the constellations of the Bear, the signs of immortal Memory.

126b.   One thing increases in one way, another in another, in relation to what it lacks.

127.   (*To the Egyptians*): 'If they are gods, why do you lament them? If you lament them, you must no longer regard them as gods.'

128.   They (*the Hellenes*) pray to statues of the gods, that do not hear them, as if they heard, and do not give, just as they cannot ask.[2]

129.   Pythagoras, son of Mnêsarchus, practised research most of all men, and making extracts from these treatises he compiled a wisdom of his own, an accumulation of learning, a harmful craft.

---

[1] For discussion, see *Companion*, pp. 128-9.
[2] Reading uncertain.

130. It is not proper to be so comic that you yourself appear comic.

131. Conceit is the regress (*hindrance*) of progress.

132. Positions of honour enslave gods and men.

133. Bad men are the adversaries of the true.

134. Education is another sun to those who are educated.

135. The shortest way to fame is to become good.

136. Souls of men slain in battle are purer than those who die of disease.

137. Utterly decreed by Fate.

138. (*Late epigram on Life: non-Heracleitean*).

139. (*Astrological forgery of Byzantine times*).

23. EPICHARMUS OF SYRACUSE

EPICHARMUS of SYRACUSE was in his prime between 485 and 467 B.C.
He wrote comedies, in which philosophical views were occasionally satirised; but these have no value for philosophy, and some of the alleged quotations are obvious forgeries: Frgs. 1-6 are almost certainly forged in support of the allegation that Plato plagiarised from Epicharmus.

1.   A   But the gods were always there, of course: they never were lacking; and these things (*probably*, '*that which is divine*') always exist in a similar form and through the same causes.

B   But still, it is said that Chaos was the first of the gods to be created.

A   How can that be? It is impossible for a 'first' thing to come from something and into something.

B   Then was there no first thing that came?

A   Certainly not! Nor a second either, at any rate of these things (*the divine?*) of which we are now speaking thus; but they were always there.

34

2.   A   Suppose to an odd number, or to an even if you like, one chooses to add a pebble or else to take one from those already there: do you think that the number remains the same?

B   No, of course not.

A   Nor, furthermore, if one chooses to add to a cubit another measure of length, or to cut off a length from what was there before: does the former measure still remain?

B   No.

A   Now look at human beings in this way: one grows, another wastes away, and all are in process of change all the time. But that which changes its nature and never remains in the same state, must also be different by now from that which has changed. So both you and I were yesterday other men, and we are other men now, and again (*we shall be*) other men (*in the future*), and never the same, according to the same Law (*Logos*).

3.   A   Is flute-playing an activity?

B   Of course.

A   Is flute-playing, then, ever a man?

B   By no means.

A   Come, let me see: what of a flute-player? What do you think he is? A man, or not?

B   Of course.

A   Then don't you think it is the same also with the Good? The Good is the activity in itself; but whoever has learnt it and knows it, he then becomes good. For just as a flute-player is one who has learnt flute-playing, or a dancer one who has learnt dancing, or a weaver weaving, or in every such example, whatever you please: he himself is not his craft, but is the craftsman.

4.   Eumaeus, wisdom is not in one thing only, but everything that lives also has understanding. For the female group hens, if you will closely observe, does not give birth to living off-spring, but sits on eggs and causes them to have life. But Nature alone knows how it is with this Wisdom, for she is self-taught.

5. It is not at all remarkable that we should speak thus of these things and should afford pleasure to ourselves and think ourselves well-endowed by nature. For dog too seems very handsome to dog, and ox to ox, and donkey very handsome to donkey, and even pig to pig.

6. As I imagine — do I really imagine? No, I know this full well, that there will be mention of these words of mine some day again. And someone will take them and strip off the metre which now they have, and give them a purple robe, embroidering it with fine phrases; and he, a man hard to throw (*in argument: metaphor from wrestling*), will show up the rest as easy to throw.

7. Well, but I do all these things under compulsion; and, I think, no one is willingly good-for-nothing or willingly accepts affliction.[1]

8. (*Epicharmus says*) the gods are winds, water, earth, sun, fire, stars; (*but I've come to the conclusion that for us the only useful gods are silver and gold*).

9. It was combined and separated, and went back to whence it came, earth to earth, breath upwards. What is difficult in this? Nothing!

10. Then what is the nature of men? Blown up bladders!

11. I don't want to die; but being dead — I don't mind that!

12. Mind sees and Mind hears; everything else is deaf and blind.

13. Keep sober and remember to be mistrustful: these are the joints of the intelligence (*i.e. what makes it supple*).

14. (*It is difficult to speak well on a poor subject*): No sooner are the words spoken than the fault appears.

15. (*By inference from Aristotle, 'Metaphysics' 1010a*): Xenophanes spoke what was unlikely, yet true.

16. That which formerly two men said, I, one man, am sufficiently (*gifted?*) to say.

---

[1] Pun on the two senses of πονηρὸς ('laden with toils' and 'wicked'), and of ἄτη ('disaster' or 'madness'); put into the mouth of Heracles in a play.

17. Character for man is good destiny — but for some men, bad also.

18. The greatest sustenance for mortals on their journey is a pious life.

19. The best thing a man can have, in my view, is health.

20. A mortal should think mortal thoughts, not immortal thoughts.

20a. Sometimes I was in the home of these men, sometimes I was with those.

21. Know how he has treated another man! . . .

22. If you are by nature pious in mind, you cannot suffer any hurt after death; your spirit will survive above in heaven.

23. Nothing escapes the divine: this you must realise. God himself is our overseer, and nothing is impossible for him.

24. Direct your thoughts as if you may live for a long time or a short time.

25. (*To stand*) surety is the daughter of folly, loss (*of money*) is the daughter of surety.

26. If you have a pure mind, you will be pure in all your body.

27. If you seek something wise, reflect during the night.

28. All serious thoughts are better discovered during the night.

29. You are not skilled at speaking: you are only incapable of keeping silent.

30. The hand washes the hand: give something and you may get something.

31. You are not generous: you have a disease — you enjoy giving.

32. Against a villain, villainy is no useless weapon.

33. Practice gives more results than a good natural endowment, my friends.

34. Who would not choose to be envied, my friends? It is obvious that a man who is not envied is of no account. One pities a blind man when one sees him, but no one envies him.

35. The virtue of the right-minded woman is not to injure her husband.

36. The gods sell all good things at the price of toil.

37. Wretch, be not mindful of what is soft, lest you have what is hard!

38. Walk towards your neighbours in a bright garment, and you will be thought by many to have intelligence, though perhaps you have none.

39. You go through everything well in word, but badly in deed.

40. To have natural endowment is best, and second best (*to learn*).

41. The wise man should think beforehand, not afterwards.

42. Do not show yourself quick to anger over trifles.

43. Not emotion, but intelligence, should be on the surface.

44. No one deliberates rightly about anything in anger.

44a. The intelligent man is (*worthy of honour?*). This is how it is: property, a house, absolute rule, wealth, strength, beauty, if they fall to a man of no intelligence, become ridiculous.

Pleasures for mortals are (*like*) impious pirates: for the man who is caught by pleasures is straightway drowned in a sea (*of them*).

45. (*Restored from a papyrus*). The man who is not at all unfortunate and has a livelihood, yet gives nothing beautiful and good to his soul, I do not call happy in the least; but rather a guardian of goods for someone else.

46. Whoever sins least, he is the best man; for no one is innocent, no one free from blame.

From the 'Epicharmus' of Ennius
47. I thought in a dream that I was dead.

48.   The body is earth, but the mind is fire.

49.   The elements are: water, earth, breath and sun.

50.   This fire (*of the soul*) is derived from the sun.

51.   And it (*the sun*) is all Mind.

52.   (*Mother Earth*) has given birth to all races in the countries, and takes them back again: (*she it is*) who gives food.

52a.   (*She is called*) Ceres, because she brings the crops.

53.   This is Jupiter, of whom I speak, whom the Greeks call Air; who is wind and clouds, and afterwards rain, and from rain comes cold, and after that, wind, and again air. Therefore these elements of which I tell you are Jupiter, because with them he helps all mortals, cities and animals.

54.   (*The 'Epicharmus' of Ennius calls the moon Proserpina too, because she is usually below the earth*).

The 'Canon' of Axiopistus
55.   (*Epicharmus gave the highest rank, among the means of divination, to dreams . . . because it is not possible to dream by free choice*).

The 'Republic' of Chrysogonus
56.   Life for mankind has great need of calculation and number. We live by calculation and number; these preserve mortals.

57.   The Law (*Logos*) steers mankind aright and ever preserves them. Man has calculation, but there is also the divine Logos. But the human Logos is sprung from the divine Logos, and it brings to each man his means of life, and his maintenance. The divine Logos accompanies all the arts, itself teaching men what they must do for their advantage; for no man has discovered any art, but it is always God.

'Chiron'
58.   And drink a double quantity of warm water, two half-measures.

58a.   A half-pound.

59.   (*Live*) birth in the eighth month is impossible.

39

60. A pugnacious ram can be tamed by boring the horns near the ears, where they curve round.

61. Afflictions of the testis and genital organs can be usefully treated by the application of a cabbage leaf.

62. Application of a wild-cabbage leaf is sufficient for the bite of a mad dog, but it is better to add silphium-juice and vinegar; dogs also die of it if it (*wild cabbage*) is given with meat.

'*Cookery*'
63. (*Half-measure*).

Epigram
64. I am a corpse. A corpse is dung, and dung is earth. If Earth is a god, then I am not a corpse but a god.

'*To Antenor*'
65. The Romans enrolled Pythagoras as a citizen.

24. ALCMAEŌN OF CROTŌN

ALCMAEŌN of CROTŌN was in his prime at the beginning of the fifth century B.C.
He wrote a book on Natural Science.

1. Alcmaeon of Croton, son of Peirithous, said the following to Brotinus and Leon and Bathyllus: concerning things unseen, (*as*) concerning things mortal, the gods have certainty, whereas to us as men conjecture (*only is possible*).

1a. Man differs from the other (*creatures*) in that he alone understands; the others perceive, but do not understand.

2. Men perish because they cannot join the beginning to the end.

3. (*In mules, the males are sterile because of the fineness and coldness of the seed, and the females because their wombs do not open*).

4. *Health is the* equality of rights *of the functions, wet-dry, cold-hot, bitter-sweet and the rest; but* single rule *among them causes disease; the single rule of either pair is deleterious. Disease*

occurs sometimes from an internal cause such as excess of heat or cold, sometimes from an external cause such as excess or deficiency of food, sometimes in a certain part, such as blood, marrow or brain; but these parts also are sometimes affected by external causes, such as certain waters or a particular site or fatigue or constraint or similar reasons. But health is the harmonious mixture of the qualities.

5. It is easier to guard against an enemy than against a friend.

25-27. ICCUS, PARÔN, AMEINIAS

ICCUS, PARÔN, AMEINIAS.
Pythagoreans: left no writings.

28. PARMENIDES OF ELEA

PARMENIDES of ELEA was in his prime about 475 B.C.
He wrote a poem in hexameter verse, addressed to his pupil Zeno; it was divided into three parts: the Prologue, the Way of Truth, the Way of Opinion.

1. The mares which carry me conveyed me as far as my desire reached, when the goddesses who were driving had set me on the famous highway which bears a man who has knowledge through all the cities. Along this way I was carried; for by this way the exceedingly intelligent mares bore me, drawing the chariot, and the maidens directed the way. The axle in the naves gave forth a pipe-like sound as it glowed (for it was driven round by the two whirling circles (*wheels*) at each end) whenever the maidens, daughters of the Sun, having left the Palace of Night, hastened their driving towards the light, having pushed back their veils from their heads with their hands.
There (*in the Palace of Night*) are the gates of the paths of Night and Day, and they are enclosed with a lintel above and a stone threshold below. The gates themselves are filled with great folding doors; and of these Justice, mighty to punish, has the interchangeable keys. The maidens, skilfully cajoling her with soft words, persuaded her to push back the bolted

bar without delay from the gates; and these, flung open, revealed a wide gaping space, having swung their jambs, richly-wrought in bronze, reciprocally in their sockets. This way, then, straight through them went the maidens, driving chariot and mares along the carriage-road.

And the goddess received me kindly, and took my right hand in hers, and thus she spoke and addressed me:

'Young man, companion of immortal charioteers, who comest by the help of the steeds which bring thee to our dwelling: welcome! — since no evil fate has despatched thee on thy journey by this road (for truly it is far from the path trodden by mankind); no, it is divine command and Right. Thou shalt inquire into everything: both the motionless heart of well-rounded Truth, and also the opinions of mortals, in which there is no true reliability. But nevertheless thou shalt learn these things (*opinions*) also — how one should go through all the things-that-seem, without exception, and test them.[1]

2. Come, I will tell you — and you must accept my word when you have heard it — the ways of inquiry which alone are to be thought: the one that IT IS, and it is not possible for IT NOT TO BE, is the way of credibility, for it follows Truth; the other, that IT IS NOT, and that IT is bound NOT TO BE: this I tell you is a path that cannot be explored; for you could neither recognise that which IS NOT, nor express it.

3. For it is the same thing to think and to be.[2]

4. Observe nevertheless how things absent are securely present to the mind; for it will not sever Being from its connection with Being, whether it is scattered everywhere utterly throughout the universe, or whether it is collected together.

5. It is all the same to me from what point I begin, for I shall return again to this same point.

[1] Reading δοκιμῶσ' (= δοκιμῶσαι) with Diels, *Vors.*, Edn. 4, and not with Kranz (Wilamowitz) δοκιμῶς (*Vors.*, 5). Wilamowitz took περῶντα with τὰ δοκοῦντα, and translated: ('Still, you shall learn these things too), how phenomena had to be on a plausible footing, because these extend throughout everything.' This interpretation is favoured by those who accept the view that Parmenides left the door open for 'Opinion' in some form; it was rejected by Diels, *Vors.* 4, Nachträge, p. xxviii, as contrary to Parmenidean metaphysic. See *Companion*, pp. 141 *sqq.*

[2] Or, reading ἔστιν: 'that which it is possible to think is identical with that which can Be'. (Zeller and Burnet, probably rightly).

6. One should both say and think that Being Is; for To Be is possible, and Nothingness is not possible. This I command you to consider; for from the latter way of search first of all I debar you. But next I debar you from that way along which wander mortals knowing nothing, two-headed,[1] for perplexity in their bosoms steers their intelligence astray, and they are carried along as deaf as they are blind, amazed, uncritical hordes, by whom To Be and Not To Be are regarded as the same and not the same, and (*for whom*) in everything there is a way of opposing stress.[2]

7, 8. For this (*view*) can never predominate, that That Which Is Not exists. You must debar your thought from this way of search, nor let ordinary experience in its variety force you along this way, (*namely, that of allowing*) the eye, sightless as it is, and the ear, full of sound, and the tongue, to rule; but (*you must*) judge by means of the Reason (*Logos*) the much-contested proof which is expounded by me.

There is only one other description of the way remaining, (*namely*), that (*What Is*) Is. To this way there are very many sign-posts: that Being has no coming-into-being and no destruction, for it is whole of limb, without motion, and without end. And it never Was, nor Will Be, because it Is now, a Whole all together, One, continuous; for what creation of it will you look for? How, whence (*could it have*) sprung? Nor shall I allow you to speak or think of it as springing from Not-Being; for it is neither expressible nor thinkable that What-Is-Not Is. Also, what necessity impelled it, if it did spring from Nothing, to be produced later or earlier? Thus it must Be absolutely, or not at all. Nor will the force of credibility ever admit that anything should come into being, beside Being itself, out of Not-Being. So far as that is concerned, Justice has never released (*Being*) in its fetters and set it free either to come into being or to perish, but holds it fast. The decision on these matters depends on the following: IT-IS, or IT IS NOT. It is therefore decided — as is inevitable — (*that one must*) ignore the one way as unthinkable and inexpressible (for it is no true way) and take the other as the way of Being and Reality. How could Being perish? How could it come into being? If it came into being, it Is Not; and so too if it is

---

[1] *i.e.*, 'in two minds'.   [2] Cp. Heracleitus, Frg. 8,

about-to-be at some future time. Thus Coming-into-Being is quenched, and Destruction also into the unseen.[1]

. Nor is Being divisible, since it is all alike. Nor is there anything (*here or*) there which could prevent it from holding together, nor any lesser thing, but all is full of Being. Therefore it is altogether continuous; for Being is close to Being.

But it is motionless in the limits of mighty bonds, without beginning, without cease, since Becoming and Destruction have been driven very far away, and true conviction has rejected them. And remaining the same in the same place, it rests by itself and thus remains there fixed; for powerful Necessity holds it in the bonds of a Limit, which constrains it round about, because it is decreed by divine law that Being shall not be without boundary. For it is not lacking; but if it were (*spatially infinite*), it would be lacking everything.[2]

To think is the same as the thought that It Is; for you will not find thinking without Being, in (*regard to*) which there is an expression. For nothing else either is or shall be except Being, since Fate has tied it down to be a whole and motionless; therefore all things that mortals have established, believing in their truth, are just a name: Becoming and Perishing, Being and Not-Being, and Change of position, and alteration of bright colour.

. But since there is a (*spatial*) Limit, it is complete on every side, like the mass of a well-rounded sphere, equally balanced from its centre in every direction; for it is not bound to be at all either greater or less in this direction or that; nor is there Not-Being which could check it from reaching to the same point, nor is it possible for Being to be more in this direction, less in that, than Being, because it is an inviolate whole. For, in all directions equal to itself, it reaches its limits uniformly.

At this point I cease my reliable theory (*Logos*) and thought, concerning Truth; from here onwards you must learn the opinions of mortals, listening to the deceptive order of my words.

They have established (*the custom of*) naming two forms, one of which ought not to be (*mentioned*): that is where they have gone astray. They have distinguished them as opposite in

---

[1] ἄπυστος, 'beyond perception'; also ἄπαυστος, 'never-ending'.
[2] Reading and meaning doubtful. Diels-Kranz: 'if it lacked Limit, it would fall short of being a Whole', but without any certainty.

form, and have marked them off from another by giving them different signs: on one side the flaming fire in the heavens, mild, very light (*in weight*), the same as itself in every direction, and not the same as the other. This (*other*) also is by itself and opposite; dark Night, a dense and heavy body. This world-order I describe to you with all its phenomena, in order that no intellect of mortal-men may outstrip you.[1]

9. But since all things are named Light and Night, and names have been given to each class of things according to the power of one or the other (*Light or Night*), everything is full equally of Light and invisible Night, as both are equal, because to neither of them belongs any share (of the other).[2]

10. You shall know the nature of the heavens, and all the signs in the heavens, and the destructive works of the pure bright torch of the sun, and whence they came into being. And you shall learn of the wandering works of the round-faced moon, and its nature; and you shall know also the surrounding heaven, whence it sprang and how Necessity brought and constrained it to hold the limits of the stars.

11. (*I will describe*) how earth and sun and moon, and the heavens common to all, and the Milky Way in the heavens, and outermost Olympus, and the hot power of the stars, hastened to come into being.

12. For the narrower rings were filled with unmixed Fire, and those next to them with Night, but between (*these*) rushes the portion of Flame. And in the centre of these is the goddess who guides everything; for throughout she rules over cruel Birth and Mating, sending the female to mate with the male, and conversely again the male with the female.

13. First of all the gods she devised Love.

14. (*The moon*): Shining by night with a light not her own, wandering round the earth.

15. (*The moon*): Always gazing towards the rays of the sun.

---

[1] Or, reading γνώμη (Stein): 'in order that no mortal may outstrip you in intelligence'.
[2] Kranz takes ἐπεί with the previous line, and translates: 'For nothing is possible which does not come under either of the two' (*i.e.* everything belongs to one or other of the two categories Light and Night).

15a.   (*Earth*): Rooted in water.

16.   For according to the mixture of much-wandering limbs which each man has, so is the mind which is associated with mankind: for it is the same thing which thinks, namely the constitution of the limbs in men, all and individually; for it is excess (*of the Light or Night-element*) which makes Thought.

17.   On the right, boys, on the left, girls . . . (*in the womb*).

18.   When a woman and a man mix the seeds of Love together, the power (*of the seeds*) which shapes (*the embryo*) in the veins out of different blood can mould well-constituted bodies only if it preserves proportion. For if the powers war (*with each other*) when the seed is mixed, and do not make a unity in the body formed by the mixture, they will terribly harass the growing (*embryo*) through the twofold seed of the (*two*) sexes.

19.   Thus, therefore, according to opinion, were these things created, and are now, and shall hereafter from henceforth grow and then come to an end. And from these things men have established a name as a distinguishing mark for each.

Doubtful
20.   But below it (*Earth?*) is a path, dreadful, hollow, muddy; this is the best path to lead one to the lovely grove of much-revered Aphrodite.

Spurious
21.   (*The moon*): Of false appearance.

22.   'Remarkably hard to convince'. (=PLATO, *Parmenides*, 135A).

23.   (*The Acropolis of Boeotian Thebes was called in ancient times 'Islands of the Blest'.*)

24.   (*The Telchînes were created from the hounds of Actaeon, which were changed into men by Zeus*).

25.   (=Empedocles, *Frg.* 28).

29. ZĒNŌ OF ELEA

Zēnō of Elea was in his prime about 450 B.C.

He wrote a book of *Epicheirêmata* (*Attacks*) in defence of Parmenides' theory of Being as One and Indivisible; his method was to take the opposite proposition that Things are Many, and derive two contradictory conclusions therefrom.

1. (*Second half of the Epicheirêma showing that if Things are Many, they must be* (a) *infinitely small,* (b) *infinitely great*).

If Being had no size, it could not Be either.

If anything Is, it follows that each (*part*) must have a certain size and bulk, and distance one from the other. And the same reasoning applies also to the part preceding it; for that too will have size and there will be another part preceding it. The same reasoning, in fact, applies always: no part of the Whole will be such as to be outermost, nor will any part be unrelated to another part. Therefore, if Things are Many, they must be both small and great: so small as to have no size, so large as to be infinite.

2. (*First half of the Epicheirêma showing that if Things are Many they must be* (a) *infinitely small,* (b) *infinitely great*).

If it (*a unit without magnitude*) be added to another existing thing, it would not make the latter at all larger. For if a thing without magnitude is added (*to another thing*) the latter cannot gain anything in magnitude. And thus (*it follows*) at once that the thing added is nothing. And if when a unit is subtracted the other will not become at all less, and will not, on the other hand, increase when (*this unit*) is added, it is clear that the unit added or subtracted was nothing.

3. (*Epicheirêma showing that if Things are Many, they must be* (a) *finite,* (b) *infinite in number*).

If Things are Many, they must be as many as they are and neither more nor less than this. But if they are as many as they are, they must be finite (*in number*).

If Things are Many, they are infinite in number. For there are always other things between those that are, and again others between those. And thus things are infinite (*in number*).

4. (*From an Epicheirêma showing the impossibility of motion*).

That which moves, moves neither in the place in which it is, nor in that in which it is not.

MELISSUS of SAMOS was in his prime about 440 B.C.

He wrote a treatise *On Being*, in defence of Parmenides' theory.

1. That which was, was always and always will be. For if it had come into being, it necessarily follows that before it came into being, Nothing existed. If however Nothing existed, in no way could anything come into being out of nothing.

2. Since therefore it did not come into being, it Is and always was and always will be, and has no beginning or end, but it is eternal. For if it had come into being, it would have a beginning (for it would have come into being at some time, and so begun), and an end (for since it had come into being, it would have ended). But since it has neither begun nor ended, it always was and always will be and has no beginning nor end. For it is impossible for anything to Be, unless it Is completely.

3. But as it Is always, so also its size must always be infinite.

4. Nothing that has a beginning and an end is either everlasting or infinite.

5. If it were not One, it will form a boundary in relation to something else.

6. If it were infinite, it would be One; for if it were two, (*these*) could not be (*spatially*) infinite, but each would have boundaries in relation to each other.

7. (1) Thus therefore it is everlasting and unlimited and one and like throughout (*homogeneous*).

(2) And neither could it perish or become larger or change its (*inner*) arrangement, nor does it feel pain or grief. For if it suffered any of these things, it would no longer be One. For if Being alters, it follows that it is not the same, but that that which previously Was is destroyed, and that Not-Being has come into being. Hence if it were to become different by a single hair in ten thousand years, so it must be utterly destroyed in the whole of time.

(3) But it is not possible for it to be rearranged either, for the previous arrangement is not destroyed, nor does a non-existent arrangement come into being. And since it is neither increased by any addition, nor destroyed, nor changed, how

could it have undergone a rearrangement of what exists? For if it were different in any respect, then there would at once be a rearrangement.

(4) Nor does it feel pain; for it could not Be completely if it were in pain; for a thing which is in pain could not always Be. Nor has it equal power with what is healthy. Nor would it be the same if it were in pain; for it would feel pain through the subtraction or addition of something, and could no longer be the same.

(5) Nor could that which is healthy feel pain, for the Healthy — That which Is — would perish, and That which Is Not would come into being.

(6) And with regard to grief, the same reasoning applies as to pain.

(7) Nor is there any Emptiness; for the Empty is Nothing; and so that which is Nothing cannot Be. Nor does it move; for it cannot withdraw in any direction, but (all) is full. For if there were any Empty, it would have withdrawn into the Empty; but as the Empty does not exist, there is nowhere for it (Being) to withdraw.

(8) And there can be no Dense and Rare. For the Rare cannot possibly be as full as the Dense, but the Rare must at once become more empty than the Dense.

(9) The following distinction must be made between the Full and the Not-Full: if a thing has room for or admits something, it is not full; if it neither has room for nor admits anything, it is full.

(10) It (Being) must necessarily be full, therefore, if there is no Empty. If therefore it is full, it does not move.

8. (1) This argument is the greatest proof that it (Being) is One only; but there are also the following proofs:

(2) If Things were Many, they would have to be of the same kind as I say the One is. For if there is earth and water and air and fire and iron and gold, and that which is living and that which is dead, and black and white and all the rest of the things which men say are real: if these things exist, and we see and hear correctly, each thing must be of such a kind as it seemed to us to be in the first place, and it cannot change or become different, but each thing must always be what it is. But now, we say we see and hear and understand correctly,

49

(3) and it seems to us that the hot becomes cold and the cold hot, and the hard soft and the soft hard, and that the living thing dies and comes into being from what is not living, and that all things change, and that what was and what now is are not at all the same, but iron which is hard is worn away by contact[1] with the finger, and gold and stone and whatever seems to be entirely strong (*is worn away*); and that from water, earth and stone come into being. So that it comes about that we neither see nor know existing things.

(4) So these statements are not consistent with one another. For although we say that there are many things, everlasting(?), having forms and strength, it seems to us that they all alter and change from what is seen on each occasion.

(5) It is clear therefore that we have not been seeing correctly, and that those things do not correctly seem to us to be Many; for they would not change if they were real, but each would Be as it seemed to be. For nothing is stronger than that which is real.

(6) And if it changed, Being would have been destroyed, and Not-Being would have come into being. Thus, therefore, if Things are Many, they must be such as the One is.

9. If therefore Being Is, it must be One; and if it is One, it is bound not to have body. But if it had Bulk, it would have parts, and would no longer Be.

10. If Being is divided, it moves; and if it moved, it could not Be.

Spurious
11. What came into being Is now and always will be.

12. (*Graeco-Syrian collection of 'Sayings of the Philosophers'*.) *Melissus has said*: 'I am very angry about the useless work at which the living toil and weary themselves: nocturnal voyages and wearisome wanderings, in which they sail amid the tumultuous waves of the sea, and hover meanwhile constantly between death and life, and tarry abroad, far distant from their homes, only to collect gain, about which they do not know who will inherit it at their death; and they do not wish to acquire the glorious treasures of wisdom, in which they will not be disappointed, because this, while they leave it behind as a

---

[1] ὁμουρέων; also ὁμοῦ ῥέων ('changing with the finger').

heritage for their friends, yet also goes with them to the next world and never forsakes them. And those who have understanding testify to this when they say: 'Such-and-such a wise man is dead, but not his wisdom.'

31. EMPEDOCLES OF ACRAGAS

EMPEDOCLES of ACRAGAS was in his prime about 450 B.C.

He wrote two poems in hexameter verses: *On Nature*, addressed to his pupil Pausanias, and *Katharmoi* (*Purifications*), addressed to his fellow-citizens of Acragas.

ON NATURE

1. Pausanias, but you must listen, son of wise Anchites!

2. For limited·are the means of grasping (*i.e. the organs oj sense-perception*) which are scattered throughout their limbs, and many are the miseries that press in and blunt the thoughts. And having looked at (*only*) a small part of existence during their lives, doomed to perish swiftly like smoke they are carried aloft and wafted away, believing only that upon which as individuals they chance to hit as they wander in all directions; but every man preens himself on having found the Whole: so little are these things to be seen by men or to be heard, or to be comprehended by the mind! But you, since you have come here into retirement, shall learn — not more than mortal intellect can attain.

3. But, ye gods, avert from my tongue the madness of those men, and guide forth from my reverent lips a pure stream! I beseech thee also, much-wooed white-armed maiden Muse, convey (*to me*) such knowledge as divine law allows us creatures of a day to hear, driving the well-harnessed car from (*the realm of*) Piety![1]

Nor shall the flowers of honour paid to fame by mortals force you at least to accept them on condition that you rashly say more than is holy — and are thereupon enthroned on the heights of wisdom!

But come, observe with every means, to see by which way

[1] Others translate: 'Muse of such things as it is lawful for mortals to hear, escort me from the realms of Piety, driving my well-harnessed car!'

Here there is probably a gap, where Empedocles takes up his address to Pausanias again.

each thing is clear, and do not hold any (*percept of*) sight higher in credibility than (*those*) according to hearing, nor (*set*) the loud-sounding hearing above the evidence of the tongue (*taste*); nor refuse credence at all to any of the other limbs where there exists a path for perception, but use whatever way of perception makes each thing clear.

4. But it is of great concern to the lower orders to mistrust the powerful; however, as the trustworthy evidence of my Muse commands, grasp (*these things*), when my reasoned argument has been sifted in your innermost heart![1]

5. To protect it within your silent bosom.

6. Hear, first, the four roots of things: bright Zeus, and life-bearing Hera, and Aidôneus, and Nêstis who causes a mortal spring of moisture to flow with her tears.

7. (*The Elements*): uncreated.

8. And I shall tell you another thing: there is no creation of substance in any one of mortal existences, nor any end in execrable death, but only mixing and exchange of what has been mixed; and the name 'substance' (*Phusis*, '*nature*') is applied to them by mankind.

9. But men, when these (*the Elements*) have been mixed in the form of a man and come into the light, or in the form of a species of wild animals, or plants, or birds, then say that this has 'come into being'; and when they separate, this men call sad fate (*death*). The terms that Right demands they do not use; but through custom I myself also apply these names.

10. Death the Avenger.

11. Fools! — for they have no long-sighted thoughts, since they imagine that what previously did not exist comes into being, or that a thing dies and is utterly destroyed.

12. From what in no wise exists, it is impossible for anything to come into being; and for Being to perish completely is incapable of fulfilment and unthinkable; for it will always be there, wherever anyone may place it on any occasion.

---

[1] διασηθέντος (Diels), from διασήθω, 'sift'; but he translates: 'when my speech has passed through the sieve of your inward parts.' Clement read διατμηθέντος, which gives: 'when my argument has been analysed in your inner parts', a perfectly sound meaning.

13. Nor is there any part of the Whole that is empty or overfull.

14. No part of the Whole is empty; so whence could anything additional come?

15. A wise man would not conjecture such things in his heart, namely, that so long as they are alive (which they call Life), they exist, and experience bad and good fortune; but that before mortals were combined (*out of the Elements*) and after they were dissolved, they are nothing at all.

16. (*Love and Hate*): As they were formerly, so also will they be, and never, I think, shall infinite Time be emptied of these two.

17. I shall tell of a double (*process*): at one time it increased so as to be a single One out of Many; at another time again it grew apart so as to be Many out of One. There is a double creation of mortals and a double decline: the union of all things causes the birth and destruction of the one (*race of mortals*), the other is reared as the elements grow apart, and then flies asunder. And these (*elements*) never cease their continuous exchange, sometimes uniting under the influence of Love, so that all become One, at other times again each moving apart through the hostile force of Hate. Thus in so far as they have the power to grow into One out of Many, and again, when the One grows apart and Many are formed, in this sense they come into being and have no stable life; but in so far as they never cease their continuous exchange, in this sense they remain always unmoved (*unaltered*) as they follow the cyclic process.

But come, listen to my discourse! For be assured, learning will increase your understanding. As I said before, revealing the aims of my discourse, I shall tell you of a double process. At one time it increased so as to be a single One out of Many; at another time it grew apart so as to be Many out of One — Fire and Water and Earth and the boundless height of Air, and also execrable Hate apart from these, of equal weight in all directions,[1] and Love in their midst, their equal in length and breadth. Observe her with your mind, and do not sit with

---

[1] ἀπάντη (Sextus); Simplicius read ἕκαστον, which has been emended to ἑκάστῳ (Panzerbieter): 'equal in weight to each' (of the Elements).

wondering eyes! She it is who is believed to be implanted in mortal limbs also; through her they think friendly thoughts and perform harmonious actions, calling her Joy and Aphrodite. No mortal man has perceived her as she moves in and out among them. But *you* must listen to the undeceitful progress of my argument.

All these (*Elements*) are equal and of the same age in their creation; but each presides over its own office, and each has its own character, and they prevail in turn in the course of Time. And besides these, nothing else comes into being, nor does anything cease. For if they had been perishing continuously, they would Be no more; and what could increase the Whole? And whence could it have come? In what direction could it perish, since nothing is empty of these things? No, but these things alone exist, and running through one another they become different things at different times, and are ever continuously the same.

18.   Love (*Philia*).[1]

19.   Adhesive Love (*Philotês*).[1]

20.   This process is clearly to be seen throughout the mass of mortal limbs: sometimes through Love all the limbs which the body has as its lot come together into One, in the prime of flourishing life; at another time again, sundered by evil feuds, they wander severally by the breakers of the shore of life. Likewise too with shrub-plants and fish in their watery dwelling, and beasts with mountain lairs and diver-birds that travel on wings.

21.   But come, observe the following witness to my previous discourse, lest in my former statements there was any substance of which the form was missing. Observe the sun, bright to see and hot everywhere, and all the immortal things (*heavenly bodies*) drenched with its heat and brilliant light; and (*observe*) the rain, dark and chill over everything; and from the Earth issue forth things based on the soil and solid. But in (*the reign of*) Wrath they are all different in form and separate, while in (*the reign of*) Love they come together and long for one another. For from these (*Elements*) come all things that were

---

[1] Empedocles probably used *Philotês*, not *Philia*; both words mean Love in the widest sense, not merely *Eros*.

and are and will be; and trees spring up, and men and women, and beasts and birds and water-nurtured fish, and even the long-lived gods who are highest in honour. For these (*Elements*) alone exist, but by running through one another they become different; to such a degree does mixing change them.

22. For all these things — beaming Sun and Earth and Heaven and Sea — are connected in harmony with their own parts: all those (*parts*) which have been sundered from them and exist in mortal limbs. Similarly all those things which are more suitable for mixture are made like one another and united in affection by Aphrodite. But those things which differ most from one another in origin and mixture and the forms in which they are moulded are completely unaccustomed to combine, and are very baneful[1] because of the commands of Hate, in that Hate has wrought their origin.

23. As when painters decorate temple-offerings with colours — men who, following their intelligence, are well-skilled in their craft — these, when they take many-coloured pigments in their hands, and have mixed them in a harmony, taking more of some, less of another, create from them forms like to all things, making trees and men and women and animals and birds and fish nurtured in water, and even long-lived gods, who are highest in honour; so let not Deception compel your mind (*to believe*) that there is any other source for mortals, as many as are to be seen existing in countless numbers. But know this for certain, since you have the account from a divinity.[2]

24. ... Touching on summit after summit, not to follow a single path of discourse to the end.

25. For what is right can well be uttered even twice.

26. In turn they get the upper hand in the revolving cycle, and perish into one another and increase in the turn appointed by Fate. For they alone exist, but running through one another they become men and the tribes of other animals, sometimes uniting under the influence of Love into one ordered Whole, at other times again each moving apart through the hostile

---

[1] λυγρά is usually translated 'sorry', 'grieved'; but cp. *Odyssey* IV. 230: φάρμακα λυγρά.
[2] The Muse.

force of Hate, until growing together into the Whole which is One, they are quelled. Thus in so far as they have the power to grow into One out of Many, and again, when the One grows apart and Many are formed, in this sense they come into being and have no stable life; but in so far as they never cease their continuous exchange, in this sense they remain always unmoved (*unaltered*) as they follow the cyclic process.[1]

27. (*The Sphere under the dominion of Love*): Therein are articulated neither the swift limbs of the sun, nor the shaggy might of Earth, nor the sea: so firmly is it (*the Whole*) fixed in a close-set secrecy, a rounded Sphere enjoying a circular solitude.[2]

27a. There is no strife nor unseemly war in his limbs.

28. But he (*God*) is equal in all directions to himself and altogether eternal, a rounded Sphere enjoying a circular solitude.

29. For there do not start two branches from his back; (*he has*) no feet, no swift knees, no organs of reproduction; but he was a Sphere, and in all directions equal to himself.

30. But when great Hate had been nourished in its limbs, and had rushed up into honour, when the time was fulfilled which, alternating, is fixed for them (*Love and Hate*) by a broad oath...

31. For all the limbs of the god trembled in succession.

32. The joint connects two things.

33. As when fig-juice binds white milk . . .

34. Having kneaded together barley-meal with water . . .

35. But I will go back to the path of song which I formerly laid down, drawing one argument from another: that (*path which shows how*) when Hate has reached the bottommost abyss of the eddy, and when Love reaches the middle of the whirl, then in it (*the whirl*) all these things come together so as to be One — not all at once, but voluntarily uniting, some from one quarter, others from another. And as they mixed,

[1] Of this fragment, v. 3 = B17, v. 34 and B21, v. 13; vv. 5, 6 = B17, vv. 7, 8; vv. 8-12 = B17, vv. 9-13.
[2] *i.e.*, content with these conditions, self-sufficient.

there poured forth countless races of mortals. But many things stand unmixed side by side with the things mixing — all those which Hate (*still*) aloft[1] checked, since it had not yet faultlessly[2] withdrawn from the Whole to the outermost limits of the circle, but was remaining in some places, and in other places departing from the limbs (*of the Sphere*). But in so far as it went on quietly streaming out, to the same extent there was entering a benevolent immortal inrush of faultless Love. And swiftly those things became mortal which previously had experienced immortality, and things formerly unmixed became mixed, changing their paths. And as they mixed, there poured forth countless races of mortals, equipped with forms of every sort, a marvel to behold.

36. As they came together, Hate returned to the outermost (*bound*).

37. (*Fire increases Fire*), Earth increases its own substance, Aether (*increases*) Aether.

38. Come now, I will first tell you of (the sun)[3] the beginning, (*the Elements*) from which all the things we now look upon came forth into view: Earth, and the sea with many waves, and damp Air, and the Titan Aether which clasps the circle all round.

39. If the depths of the earth were unlimited, and also the vast Aether, a doctrine which has foolishly issued forth off the tongues of many, and has been spread abroad out of their mouths, since they have seen only a little of the Whole . . .

40. Sharp-shooting sun and gracious moon.

41. But (*the sun*) collected in a ball travels round the great sky.

42. (*The moon*) cuts off his (*the sun's*) rays, whenever she goes below him, and she throws a shadow on as much of the Earth as is the breadth of the bright-eyed moon.

43. Thus the ray (*of sunshine*) having struck the broad surface of the moon (*returns at once in order that, running, it may reach the heavens*).

[1] *i.e.*, not yet fallen to the bottom.
[2] *i.e.*, 'completely', so that no fault could be found with the mixture.
[3] ἥλιον Clem.; corrupt.

44. (*The Sun, having been round the Earth, by reflection from the heavenly light*) flashes back to Olympus with serene countenance.

45. There whirls round the Earth a circular borrowed light.

46. As the nave of the chariot (*-wheel*) whirls round the goal, (*so does the moon circle closely round the Earth*).

47. She gazes at the sacred circle of her lord (*the sun*) opposite.

48. It is the Earth that makes night by coming in the way of the (*sun's*) rays.

49. Of night, lonely, blind-eyed.

50. Iris brings from the sea a wind or a great rain-storm.

51. Mightily upwards (*rushes Fire*).

52. Many fires burn below the surface (*of the Earth*).

53. For so (*the Aether*) chanced to be running at that time, though often differently.

54. (*Fire by nature rose upwards*), but Aether sank down with long roots upon the Earth.

55. Sea, the sweat of Earth.

56. Salt was solidified, pressed by the forceful rays (*of the sun*).

57. On it (*Earth*) many foreheads without necks sprang forth, and arms wandered unattached, bereft of shoulders, and eyes strayed about alone, needing brows.

58. Limbs wandered alone.

59. But as the one divinity became more and more mingled with the other (*i.e. Love and Hate*), these things fell together as each chanced, and many other things in addition to these were continuously produced.

60. Creatures with rolling gait and innumerable hands.

61. Many creatures were created with a face and breast on both sides; offspring of cattle with the fronts of men, and again

there arose offspring of men with heads of cattle; and (*creatures made of elements*) mixed in part from men, in part of female sex, furnished with hairy limbs.[1]

62.　Come now, hear how the Fire as it was separated sent up the night-produced shoots of men and much-lamenting women; for my tale is not wide of the mark nor ill-informed. At first, undifferentiated shapes of earth arose, having a share of both elements Water and Heat. These the Fire sent up, wishing to reach its like, but they did not yet exhibit a lovely body with limbs, nor the voice and organ such as is proper to men.

63.　But the substance of (*the child's*) limbs is divided (*between them*), part in the man's (*body and part in the woman's*).

64.　Upon him comes Desire also, reminding[2] him through sight.

65.　And they (*male and female seed*) were poured into the pure parts. Some of it forms women, (*namely*) that which has encountered Cold, (*and conversely that which encounters Hot produces males*).

66.　The divided meadows of Aphrodite.

67.　For in the warmer part the stomach (*i.e. the womb*) is productive of the male, and for this reason men are swarthy and more powerfully built[3] and more shaggy.

68.　On the tenth day of the eighth month (*the blood*) becomes a white putrefaction (*milk*).

69.　Double-bearing: (*women, as bearing in both the seventh and the ninth months*).

70.　Sheepskin: (*the membrane, or caul, round the unborn child*).

71.　But if your belief concerning these matters was at all lacking — how from the mixture of Water, Earth, Aether and Sun (*Fire*) there came into being the forms and colours of mortal things in such numbers as now exist fitted together by Aphrodite . . .

[1] σκιεροῖς (Kranz); Diels read στείροις ('sterile').
[2] ἀναμιμνήσκων, a dubious emendation by Diels for ἀμμίσγων, 'mingling' (male and female).
[3] ἀδρομελέστεροι: Karsten for MSS. ἀνδρωδέστεροι.

72. How also tall trees and fish of the sea . . .

73. And as at that time Cypris, when she had drenched earth with rain-water, busying herself in preparation of the forms,[1] gave them to swift Fire to strengthen them . . .

74. (*Aphrodite*): bringing the tuneless tribe of prolific fish.

75. Of (*the animals*), those that are of dense composition on the outside and rare within, having received this flabbiness under the hands of Cypris . . .

76. This is (*found*) in the hard-backed shells of the sea-dwellers, especially the sea-snails and the stone-skinned turtles. There you will see earth dwelling on the surface of the flesh.

77, 78. (*Trees*) retentive of their leaves and retentive of their fruit, flourish with abundance of fruit all the year round, in accordance with the Air (*i.e. Vapour, Moisture, in their composition*).

79. Thus eggs are borne, first by the tall olive trees . . .

80. . . . Which is the reason why pomegranates are late-ripening and apples remain juicy for so long(?).[2]

81. Wine is the water from the bark, after it has fermented in the wood.

82. Hair, and leaves, and the close feathers of birds, and the scales that grow on stout limbs, are the same thing.

83. But hedgehogs have sharp-shooting hairs that bristle on their backs.

84. As when a man, thinking to make an excursion through a stormy night, prepares a lantern, a flame of burning fire, fitting lantern-plates to keep out every sort of winds, and these plates disperse the breath of the blowing winds; but the light leaps out through them, in so far as it is finer, and shines across the threshold with unwearying beams: so at that time did the aboriginal Fire, confined in membranes and in fine

---

[1] εἴδεα. Diels read ἴδεα from ἴδος (damp heat).

[2] Plutarch, who quotes this, did not know the meaning of ὑπέρφλοιον, but was told by scholars that φλοίειν is used to mean 'to be in its prime', 'to flourish', and as the apple is the fruit which best preserves its prime, the poet called it 'of surpassing or enduring ripeness'. Empedocles is explaining the effect of the sun on various fruits.

tissues, hide itself[1] in the round pupils; and these (*tissues*) were pierced throughout with marvellous passages. They kept out the deep reservoir of water surrounding the pupil, but let the Fire through (*from within*) outwards, since it was so much finer.

85. But the benevolent flame (*of the eye*) happened to obtain only a slight admixture of Earth.

86. . . . Out of which (*Elements*) divine Aphrodite built tireless eyes.

87. Aphrodite, having fastened them (*eyes*) together with clamps of affection . . .

88. One vision is produced by both (*eyes*).

89. Realising that from all created things there are effluences . . .

90. Thus sweet seized on sweet, bitter rushed towards bitter, sour moved towards sour, and hot settled upon hot.

91. (*Water is*) more able to agree with wine, but unwilling (*to mix*) with oil.

92. (*The sterility of mules is due to the quality of their seed: both the male and female seed are soft substances which when mixed produce a hard substance, as when*) brass is mixed with tin.

93. The berry of the grey elder mingles with the linen.[2]

94. And the black colour in the bottom of a river arises from the shadow, and the same thing is seen in deep caves.

95. When first they (*the eyes*) grew together in the hands of Cypris . . . (*explanation of why some creatures see better by day, others by night*).

---

[1] λοχάζετο here is intransitive. Burnet wrongly takes it as transitive and supplies 'she (Love)' as the subject. For the accusative κούρην cp. Hdt. v. 121, ἐλόχησαν ὁδόν 'occupied the road with an ambuscade'.

[2] This fragment concerns dyeing, as illustrative of the power of assimilation of one substance by another. The MSS. read κρόκου or κρόκον, for which Diels substituted κόκκος, 'berry'; and ἀκτίς, for which Wilamowitz suggested ἀκτῆς, from ἀκτέα, 'elder'. If the MSS. readings κρόκου and ἀκτίς be retained, the fragment can be more plausibly translated: 'The ray of bright(?) saffron mingles with the linen.' The emendations are ingenious but improbable.

96. But the Earth obligingly in its broad vessels received two parts out of the eight of shining Nêstis, four of Hephaestus. And these became the white bones fitted together by the cementing of Harmony, divinely originated.

97. The spine (*acquired its present form by being broken when the animal turned its neck*).

98. The Earth, having been finally moored in the harbours of Love, joined with these in about equal proportions: with Hephaestus, with moisture, and with all-shining Aether, either a little more (*of Earth*) or a little less to their more. And from these came blood and the forms of other flesh.

99. (*The ear is a kind of*) bell. (*It is*) a fleshy shoot.

100. The way everything breathes in and out is as follows: all (*creatures*) have tubes of flesh, empty of blood, which extend over the surface of the body; and at the mouths of these tubes the outermost surface of the skin is perforated with frequent pores, so as to keep in the blood while a free way is cut for the passage of the air. Thus, when the thin blood flows back from here, the air, bubbling, rushes in in a mighty wave; and when the blood leaps up (*to the surface*), there is an expiration of air. As when a girl, playing with a water-catcher[1] of shining brass — when, having placed the mouth of the pipe on her well-shaped hand she dips the vessel into the yielding substance of silvery water, still the volume of air pressing from inside on the many holes keeps out the water, until she uncovers the condensed stream (*of air*). Then at once when the air flows out, the water flows in in an equal quantity. Similarly, when water occupies the depths of the brazen vessel, and the opening or passage is stopped by the human flesh (*hand*), and the air outside, striving to get in, checks the water, by controlling the surface at the entrance of the noisy strainer[2] until she lets go with her hand:

[1] *Klepsydra:* not here the water-clock, but a domestic vessel for picking up small quantities of liquid out of a larger vessel. See Hugh Last, *Class. Q.* XVIII (1924), pp. 169 *sqq.* for description and illustration.

[2] ἤθμοῖο, the base of the water-catcher, pierced with holes through which the liquid enters. This, the reading of a few less good MSS., is probably correct. Burnet prefers the commoner ἰσθμοῖο (the control-pipe at the top of the vessel), because of δυσηχέος ('noisy'), which he thinks means 'gurgling', as when a bottle full of water is turned upside down; such an experiment is described in Aristotle, *Probl.* 914b. But this is not to the point here: the water-catcher was not turned upside down, but the flow of liquid was regulated by opening and shutting the upper entrance with the hand.

then again, in exactly the opposite way from what happened before, as the air rushes in, the water flows out in equal volume. Similarly when the thin blood, rushing through the limbs, flows back into the interior, straightway a stream of air flows in with a rush; and when the blood flows up again, again there is a breathing-out in equal volume.

101.   . . . Tracking down with its nostrils the portions of animal limbs, all those (*portions*) that, when living, they left behind from their feet on the tender grass.[1]

102.   Thus all (*creatures*) have a share of breathing and smell.

103.   Thus all (*creatures*) have intelligence, by the will of Fortune.

104.   And in so far as the rarest things came together in their fall . . .

105.   (*The heart*) nourished in the seas of blood which courses in two opposite directions: this is the place where is found for the most part what men call Thought; for the blood round the heart is Thought in mankind.

106.   The intelligence of Man grows towards the material that is present.

107.   For from these (*Elements*) are all things fitted and fixed together, and by means of these do men think, and feel pleasure and sorrow.

108.   In so far as their natures have changed (*during the day*), so does it befall men to think changed thoughts (*in their dreams*).

109.   We see Earth by means of Earth, Water by means of Water, divine Air by means of Air, and destructive Fire by means of Fire; Affection by means of Affection, Hate by means of baneful Hate.

109a.   (*Reflections are emanations on to the mirror from the objects mirrored*).

110.   If you press them (*these truths?*) deep into your firm

---

[1] The hunting-dog is referred to. Smell, an emanation from the animal, is given off only when it is alive; hence, when dead, it does not leave traces of interest to other animals.

mind, and contemplate them with good will and a studious care that is pure, these things will all assuredly remain with you throughout your life; and you will obtain many other things from them; for these things of themselves cause each (*element*) to increase in the character, according to the way of each man's nature. But if you intend to grasp after different things such as dwell among men in countless numbers and blunt their thoughts, miserable (*trifles*), certainly these things will quickly desert you in the course of time, longing to return to their own original kind. For all things, be assured, have intelligence and a portion of Thought.

111. You shall learn all the drugs that exist as a defence against illness and old age; for you alone will I accomplish all this. You shall check the force of the unwearying winds which rush upon the earth with their blasts and lay waste the cultivated fields. And again, if you wish, you shall conduct the breezes back again. You shall create a seasonable dryness after the dark rain for mankind, and again you shall create after summer drought the streams that nourish the trees and [which will flow in the sky].[1] And you shall bring out of Hades a dead man restored to strength.

KATHARMOI (PURIFICATIONS)

112. Friends, who dwell in the great town on the city's heights, looking down on yellow Acragas, you who are occupied with good deeds, who are harbours (*of refuge*) treating foreigners with respect, and who are unacquainted with wickedness: greeting! I go about among you as an immortal god, no longer a mortal, held in honour by all, as I seem (*to them to deserve*),[2] crowned with fillets and flowing garlands. When I come to them in their flourishing towns, to men and women, I am honoured; and they follow me in thousands, to inquire where is the path of advantage, some desiring oracles, while others ask to hear a word of healing for their manifold diseases, since they have long been pierced with cruel pains.

113. But why do I lay stress on these things, as if I were achieving something great in that I surpass mortal men who are liable to many forms of destruction?

---

[1] Reading corrupt.

[2] ὥσπερ ἔοικα. Diels translated this 'as I deserve', which, as Kranz says, is impossible. Another reading is ἔοικε, 'as is proper'. See *Companion*, p. 178, note.

114. Friends, I know that Truth is present in the story that I shall tell; but it is actually very difficult for men, and the impact of conviction on their minds is unwelcome.

115. There is an oracle of Necessity, an ancient decree of the gods, eternal, sealed fast with broad oaths, that when one of the divine spirits whose portion is long life sinfully stains his own limbs with bloodshed, and following Hate has sworn a false oath — these must wander for thrice ten thousand seasons far from the company of the blessed, being born throughout the period into all kinds of mortal shapes, which exchange one hard way of life for another. For the mighty Air chases them into the Sea, and the Sea spews them forth on to the dry land, and the Earth (*drives them*) towards the rays of the blazing Sun; and the Sun hurls them into the eddies of the Aether. One (*Element*) receives them from the other, and all loathe them. Of this number am I too now, a fugitive from heaven and a wanderer, because I trusted in raging Hate.

116. (*The Grace*) loathes intolerable Necessity.

117. For by now I have been born as boy, girl, plant, bird, and dumb sea-fish.

118. I wept and wailed when I saw the unfamiliar land (*at birth*).

119. How great the honour, how deep the happiness from which (*I am exiled*)!

120. 'We have come into this roofed cavern.' (*Spoken by those who escort the souls to Earth*).

121. ... The joyless land where are Murder and Wrath and the tribes of other Dooms, and Wasting Diseases and Corruptions and the Works of Dissolution[1] wander over the Meadow of Disaster in the darkness.

122. Here were the Earth-Mother (Chthoniê) and the far-seeing Sunshine-Nymph (Hêliopê), bloody Discord, and Harmony with her serious mien, Beauty and Ugliness, the

---

[1] ἔργα τε ῥευστά. Diels (followed by Burnet) thought that this referred to floods; but bodily ailments are here in question. Bignone suggested 'works of dissolution'. Kranz translates 'the work of Rheuma', *i.e.* of diseases due to excess of the moist element, as opposed to fevers ('wasting diseases').

Speed-Nymph and the Nymph of Delay; and lovely Infallibility and dark-eyed Uncertainty.

123. (*The female figures*) Growth and Decay, Rest and Waking, Movement and Immobility, much-crowned Majesty, and Defilement, Silence and Voice.

124. Alas, oh wretched race of mortals, direly unblessed! Such are the conflicts and groanings from which you have been born!

125. For from living creatures he made them dead, changing their forms, (*and from dead, living*).

126. (*A female divinity*) clothing (*the soul*) in the unfamiliar tunic of flesh.

127. In the (*realm of*) animals they become lions that have their lair in the mountains, and their bed on the ground; and in (*the realm of*) fair-tressed trees, (*they become*) laurels.

128. And for them there was no god Ares, nor Battle-Din, nor Zeus the King, nor Cronos nor Poseidon, but only Cypris the Queen. These men sought to please her with pious gifts — with painted animals and perfumes of cunningly-devised smell, with sacrifice of unmixed myrrh and of fragrant incense, and by casting libations of yellow honey on the ground. And the altar was not drenched with the unmixed blood of bulls, but this was the greatest pollution among men, to devour the goodly limbs (*of animals*) whose life they had reft from them.

129. There was living among them a man of surpassing knowledge, who had acquired the extremest wealth of the intellect, one expert in every kind of skilled activity. For whenever he reached out with his whole intellect, he easily discerned each one of existing things, in ten and even twenty lifetimes of mankind.

130. And all creatures, both animals and birds, were tame and gentle towards men, and friendliness glowed between them.

131. If for the sake of any mortal, immortal Muse, it has pleased thee that my poetic endeavours should be of concern

to thee, now once again, in answer to my prayer, stand beside me, Calliopeia, as I expound a good theory concerning the blessed gods!

132. Happy is he who has acquired the riches of divine thoughts, but wretched the man in whose mind dwells an obscure opinion about the gods!

133. It is not possible to bring God near within reach of our eyes, nor to grasp him with our hands, by which route the broadest road of Persuasion runs into the human mind.

134. For he is not equipped with a human head on his body, nor from his back do two branches start; (he has) no feet, no swift knees,[1] no hairy genital organs; but he is Mind, holy and ineffable, and only Mind, which darts through the whole universe with its swift thoughts.

135. But that which is lawful for all extends continuously through the broad-ruling Air and through the boundless Light.[2]

136. Will ye not cease from this harsh-sounding slaughter? Do you not see that you are devouring one another in the thoughtlessness of your minds?

137. The father having lifted up the son slaughters him with a prayer, in his great folly. But they are troubled[3] at sacrificing one who begs for mercy. But he, on the other hand, deaf to (the victim's) cries, slaughters him in his halls and prepares the evil feast. Likewise son takes father, and children their mother, and tearing out the life, eat the flesh of their own kin.

138. Having drained off their life with bronze . . .

139. (Hymn of repentance for sins of diet): 'Alas that a pitiless day did not destroy me before I planned evil deeds of eating with my lips!'

140. Keep entirely away from laurel-leaves!

[1] vv. 1, 2,=B29, vv. 1, 2.
[2] Divine law as opposed to human law; said to refer in particular to the prohibition of animal-slaughter.
[3] οἱ δ' ἀπορεῦνται, emendation of Diels, who takes 'they' as 'the attendants at the sacrifice'. If the MSS. reading οἱ δὲ πορεῦνται λισσόμενοι be retained, the meaning is: 'they (the victims) come up to beg for mercy'.

141. Wretches, utter wretches, keep your hands off beans!

142. Him will the roofed palace of aegis-bearing Zeus never receive, nor yet the roof of Hades and of the piteous voice.[1]

143. (*Wash the hands*) cutting off (*water*) from five springs into (*a vessel of*) enduring bronze.

144. To fast from sin.

145. Therefore you are distraught with dire sins, and shall never ease your heart of your grievous sorrows!

146. And at the last they become seers, and bards, and physicians, and princes among earth-dwelling men, from which (*state*) they blossom forth as gods highest in honour.

147. Sharing the hearth of the other immortals, sharing the same table, freed from the lot of human griefs, indestructible.

148. Earth that envelops mortals (*the body*).

149. Cloud-gathering Air.

150. Full-blooded liver.[2]

151. Life-giving Aphrodite.

152. (*Old age, the evening of life; evening, the old age of the day: a similar metaphor in Empedocles*)

153. Baubô.[3]

153a. In seven times seven days (*the unborn child is formed*).

Doubtful fragments
154. (*Plutarch, 'On Eating Flesh', has a passage in defence of those who began the practice: they did not do it out of lawless self-indulgence, but from dire need. He imagines them addressing the men of today and saying: 'You have plenty of everything; but for us life was hard. It was a time before*) the sun had settled in his unchanging course, so as to divide morning and evening; before his path turned back again, crowning him with the

---

[1] An uncertain restoration by Diels of a passage quoted for grammatical reasons, from the Herculanean MSS.

[2] Quoted by Plutarch to show that Empedocles does not use epithets idly for the sake of fine writing, but in order to bring out the exact nature or function of something.

[3] Connected with Demeter in Orphic mythology; said to have been used by Empedocles to mean 'belly'.

fruit-bearing, flower-garlanded seasons; when the Earth was overwhelmed with the unregulated outpourings of rivers, and vast areas were deserts, formless because of lakes, deep mud-pits, barren scrub and woodland.'

154a. A potion of birth-pangs, pains, disappointments and lamentations . . .

154b. (ARATUS, *Phaenomena,* 131 *sqq.*)

154c. It is immediately clear which plants are going to be-fruitful.

Spurious fragments
155.. Têlaugês, famous son of Theanô and Pythagoras!

156. (*Elegiac verses on Pausanias, the pupil to whom the poem 'On Nature' is addressed*).

157. (*Punning elegiac couplet on Acrôn, a physician of Acragas*).

158. Bereaved of the happy life.

159. The accumulated bulk.

32. MENESTÔR OF SYBARIS

MENESTÔR of SYBARIS was in his prime about the middle of the fifth century. He wrote on botany, but none of his writings has survived. His opinions are quoted by Theophrastus.

33. XUTHUS

XUTHUS. A Pythagorean. He left no writings.

34. BOÏDAS

BOÏDAS. Time and place unknown. He left no writings.

35. THRASYALCES OF THASOS

THRASYALCES of THASOS. An early meteorologist. No writings have survived.

36. IŌN OF CHIOS

IŌN of CHIOS was active between 452 and 421 B.C.

He wrote tragedies, lyrics and other poems; also a philosophical work in prose called *Triagmos* ('*Triad*') or *Triagmoi*.

1.   The beginning of my work is: everything is Three and nothing more or less than these three. The virtue of each thing is a Triad: intelligence, strength, luck.

2.   (*Pythagoras ascribed some of his writings to Orpheus*).

3.   Luck, that differs greatly from Art, creates many things that are like it.

3a   (*The twenty-fifth letter is called Agma*).

3b.   (*Of men*) agreeing in their views and sharing the same libations.

4.   Thus Pherecydes, who was outstanding in manliness and reverence, even after death has a joyful life for his soul, if the wise Pythagoras had insight concerning all men and knew (*them*) thoroughly.

Dubious fragment

5.   Eleven-stringed lyre, which hast a ten-intervalled range, for a triple melodious way of harmony, before thee the Hellenes used to play a lyre of seven strings with (*only*) a tetrachord, creating a thin music!

37. DAMŌN OF ATHENS

DAMŌN of ATHENS was in his prime about 460 B.C.

His teaching seems to have been mainly oral, but he is said to have incorporated his doctrines in an *Areopagiticus* (speech purporting to be written for delivery to the Areopagus).

1.   (CICERO: *Damon treated music in a way that embraced not merely the particular but the universal*).

2.   (PHILODEMUS: *If Damon addressed the actual, and not a fictitious Areopagus, he deceived them in saying that men of taste should take up music*).

3.   Those who practise the licentious sport . . .

4. (PHILODEMUS: *If anyone inquires whether music advances one in all the virtues or only in some, the answer is given that Damon thinks that it is in all, for he says*): in singing and playing the lyre, a boy will be likely to reveal not only Courage and Moderation, but also Justice.

5. (Ps.-PLUTARCH: *The relaxed Lydian mode was discovered by Damon*).

6. Song and dance necessarily arise when the soul is in some way moved; liberal and beautiful songs and dances create a similar soul, and the reverse kind create a reverse kind of soul.

7. (ARISTEIDES QUINTILIANUS: *Through similarity, the notes of a continuous melody create a character that did not exist in boys and in those more advanced in years, and also bring out the latent character. This was the doctrine of Damon's school also. In the harmonies handed down by him it is possible to find in the sequences of notes that sometimes the female notes, sometimes the male, either predominate or diminish or are completely absent, obviously because a different harmony was serviceable according to the character of each particular soul*).

8. (SOCRATES *in the 'Laches' of* Plato: *Damon has much in common with Prodicus, who excelled in the science of nomenclature*).

9. (SOCRATES *in the 'Republic' of* Plato: *Socrates pretends to have an uncertain recollection of Damon's teaching, in which Damon analysed metres and their feet, using terms such as 'martial', 'dactylic', 'heroic', and described the iambus and the trochee; he assigned praise and blame not only to the rhythms for moral quality, but also to the feet, or to both together*).

10. Musical modes are nowhere altered without (*changes in*) the most important laws of the State.

38. HIPPÔN OF SAMOS

HIPPÔN of SAMOS flourished during the middle of the fifth century B.C.
He published his views in several books; but only one genuine fragment has survived.

1. All water that is drunk comes from the sea; for of course

the wells from which we drink are not deeper than the sea, for in that case the water would not be from the sea but from elsewhere. But in fact the sea is deeper than the water. It follows therefore that all water that is above the sea comes from the sea.

Spurious

2. (*Elegiac epitaph on himself, claiming apotheosis*).

3. Nothing is more empty than much learning.

4. The soul is very different from the body: it is active when the body is inert, it sees when the body is blind and lives when the body is dead.

39. PHALEAS OF CHALCÊDÔN AND HIPPODÂMUS OF MILÊTUS

PHALEAS of CHALCÊDÔN: exact date unknown.
HIPPODÂMUS of MILÊTUS: active during the middle of the fifth century B.C.
No writings survive.

40. POLYCLEITUS OF ARGOS

POLYCLEITUS of ARGOS was active during the latter half of the fifth century B.C.
He wrote a treatise called *Canon*, on aesthetics.

1. The most difficult stage of the work is when the artists' clay is within a nail's breadth[1] (*of completion?*)

2. The right result comes gradually through many numbers.

41. OENOPIDES OF CHIOS

OENOPIDES of CHIOS was active during the latter half of the fifth century B.C.
No writings survive.

[1] Proverbial expression, the meaning of which is uncertain.

42. HIPPOCRATES OF CHIOS

HIPPOCRATES of CHIOS flourished during the latter half of the fifth century B.C.

(AESCHYLUS was the name of one of his pupils).

He was the first to write a text-book of mathematics, called the *Elements*. Parts of it were incorporated by Simplicius in his Commentary on the *Physics* of Aristotle; but the work itself is lost.

43. THEODÔRUS OF CYRÊNÊ

THEODÔRUS of CYRÊNÊ: latter half of fifth century B.C.

He appears as a speaker in three of Plato's dialogues; but no writings of his survive.

44. PHILOLÂUS OF TARENTUM

PHILOLÂUS of TARENTUM was active in the latter half of the fifth century B.C.

He was said to have written one book, which was the first published account of Pythagoreanism. The fragments attributed to him are in Doric dialect. Their genuineness has been disputed by modern scholars, probably without justification.[1] This work was usually given the title *On the Universe*. Another work entitled *Bacchae* was sometimes attributed to him.

1. Nature in the universe was fitted together from the Non-Limited and the Limiting, both the universe as a whole and everything in it.

2. All existing things must necessarily be either Limiting, or Non-Limited, or both Limiting and Non-Limited. But they could not be merely Non-Limited (nor merely Limited). Since however it is plain that they are neither wholly from the Limiting nor wholly from the Non-Limited, clearly then the universe and its contents were fitted together from both the Limiting and the Non-Limited. This is proved also by actual existing things; for those of them which are made of Limiting (*elements*) impose Limit, whereas those made of both Limiting and Non-Limited (*elements*) both do and do not impose Limit, and those made of Non-Limited (*elements*) will appear Non-Limited.

[1] See *Companion*, pp. 228-9.

3. For there could not even be an object set before knowledge to begin with, if all things were Non-Limited.

4. Actually, everything that can be known has a Number; for it is impossible to grasp anything with the mind or to recognise it without this (*Number*).

5. Actually, Number has two distinct forms, odd and even, and a third compounded of both, the even-odd; each of these two forms has many aspects, which each separate object demonstrates in itself.

6. This is how it is with Nature and Harmony: the Being of things is eternal, and Nature itself requires divine and not human intelligence; moreover, it would be impossible for any existing thing to be even recognised by us if there did not exist the basic Being of the things from which the universe was composed, (*namely*) both the Limiting and the Non-Limited. But since these Elements exist as unlike and unrelated, it would clearly be impossible for a universe to be created with them unless a harmony was added, in which way this (*harmony*) did come into being. Now the things which were like and related needed no harmony; but the things which were unlike and unrelated and unequally arranged are necessarily fastened together by such a harmony, through which they are destined to endure in the universe. . . .

The content of the Harmony (*Octave*) is the major fourth and the major fifth; the fifth is greater than the fourth by a whole tone; for from the highest string (*lowest note*) to the middle is a fourth, and from the middle to the lowest string (*highest note*) is a fifth. From the lowest to the third string is a fourth, from the third to the highest string is a fifth. Between the middle and third strings is a tone. The major fourth has the ratio 3:4, the fifth 2:3, and the octave 1:2. Thus the Harmony (*Octave*) consists of five whole tones and two semitones, the fifth consists of three tones and a semitone, and the fourth consists of two tones and a semitone.

7. The first composite (*entity*), the One, which is in the centre of the Sphere, is called Hearth.

8. The One is the beginning of everything.

9. By nature, not by convention.

74

10.   Harmony is a Unity of many mixed (*elements*), and an agreement between disagreeing (*elements*).

11.   One must study the activities and the essence of Number in accordance with the power existing in the Decad (*Ten-ness*); for it (*the Decad*) is great, complete, all-achieving, and the origin of divine and human life and its Leader; it shares ... The power also of the Decad. Without this, all things are unlimited, obscure and indiscernible.

For the nature of Number is the cause of recognition, able to give guidance and teaching to every man in what is puzzling and unknown. For none of existing things would be clear to anyone, either in themselves or in their relationship to one another, unless there existed Number and its essence. But in fact Number, fitting all things into the soul through sense-perception, makes them recognisable and comparable with one another as is provided by the nature of the Gnômôn,[1] in that Number gives them body and divides the different relationships of things, whether they be Non-Limited or Limiting, into their separate groups.

And you may see the nature of Number and its power at work not only in supernatural and divine existences but also in all human activities and words everywhere, both throughout all technical production and also in music.

The nature of Number and Harmony admits of no Falsehood; for this is unrelated to them. Falsehood and Envy belong to the nature of the Non-Limited and the Unintelligent and the Irrational.

Falsehood can in no way breathe on Number; for Falsehood is inimical and hostile to its nature, whereas Truth is related to and in close natural union with the race of Number.

12.   The bodies (*physical Elements*) of the Sphere are five: the Fire in the Sphere, and the Water, and Earth, and Air, and, fifth, the vehicle(?)[2] of the Sphere.

13.   (*The Four Elements of the rational animal are: Brain, Heart, Navel, Genital Organ*). The Head is the seat of the Mind, the

---

[1] Gnômôn: here, a figure used in solving geometrical problems. Heath, *Greek Mathematics*, I. p. 78; and Newbold, *Philolaus*, in *Arch. für Gesch. der Phil.* (1906) pp. 176 *sqq.*

[2] ὁλκάς, 'hull of a ship'; some emend to ὁλκός, 'roll' or 'envelope', an unlikely meaning.

Heart of the Soul and of feeling, the Navel of the Rooting and Growth of the original (*embryo*), the Genital Organ of the emission of Seed and of Creation. The Brain (indicates) the ruling factor of Man, the Heart that of the animal, the Navel that of the plant, and the Genital Organ of them all; for they all derive their life and growth from a seed.

14. The ancient theologians and seers also bear witness that because of certain punishments the soul is yoked to the body and buried in it as in a tomb.

15. (*Socrates to Cebes in the 'Phaedo':-The theory that we are in a sort of watch-tower which we must not desert is difficult; but I agree that we are one of the possessions of the gods*).[1]

16. There are certain thoughts which are stronger than ourselves.

Attributed to a prose work called 'Bacchae'
17. (STOBAEUS: *paraphrase*). The universe is one, and it began to come into being from the centre, and from the centre upwards at the same intervals (*of distance*) as those below. For the parts above from the centre are in inverse relationship to those below; for the centre is to what is below as it is to what is above, and so with all the rest; for both stand in the same relationship to the centre, except in so far as their positions are reversed.

18. (STOBAEUS: *quotation on the Sun has fallen out*).

19. (PROCLUS: *Plato, Pythagorean doctrine and Philolaus in the 'Bacchae' teach theology through mathematical figures*).

Doubtful fragments
20. (*The Number Seven is like*) Nikê (*i.e. Athena*), the Motherless and Virgin . . . for it is ruler and teacher of all things; it is God, One ever-existing, stable, unmoving, itself like to itself, different from the rest.

20a. The Dyad (*Two-ness*) is the Bride of Cronos.

Spurious fragments
21. (*Quoted by Stobaeus from a work attributed to Philolaus entitled 'On the Soul'*).

---

[1] Plato does not name Philolaus here; but his name is applied by Athenagoras (second century A.D.) to a similar statement.

Therefore it (the universe) endures both indestructible and indomitable for endless time. For neither within it will there be found any cause more powerful than itself, nor outside it any cause able to destroy it. But this universe was from eternity and will endure till eternity, One, steered by One, akin to it and most powerful and unsurpassable. The universe, being one and continuous and inspired by the breath of Nature and carried round, has also the beginning of motion and change from its first beginning. And part of it is unchanging and part changing. And the unchanging part has its bounds from the Soul which encloses the Whole as far as the moon; and the changing part from the moon to the earth. But since the moving part circles from everlasting to everlasting, and the part that is moved is disposed in whatever way the moving part carries it, it follows necessarily that one is ever in motion and the other ever passive. And the one is wholly the dwelling (?) of Mind and Soul, and the other of Becoming and Change; and the one is first in power and superior, and the other is second and inferior. But that which is made of both these, namely the ever-running (*circling*) Divine and the ever-changing Mortal, is the universe.

It is well that the universe should be an everlasting activity of God and Becoming, according to the attendance (*on God*) of changeable Nature. And he remains One for ever in the same position and condition, but particular existences are coming into being and perishing in vast numbers. And they, when given over to destruction, yet keep their natures and forms, and in birth they reproduce the same form as their father and creator who gave them birth . . .

22. (CLAUDIANUS MAMERTUS (*5th century A.D.*) *purporting to quote from the third volume of a treatise of Philolaus 'On Rhythm and Metre').*
The soul is joined to the body through Number and the immortal and likewise incorporeal Harmony . . . The body is loved by the soul, because without it it cannot use the senses. When the soul has been separated from the body by death, it lives an incorporeal existence in the world.

23. (IAMBLICHUS) Number is the ruling and self-created bond which maintains the everlasting stability of the contents of the universe.

45. EURYTUS OF SOUTHERN ITALY

EURYTUS of SOUTHERN ITALY: about 400 B.C.
No writings survive.

46. ARCHIPPUS AND LÝSIS OF TARENTUM; OPSIMUS OF RHÊGIUM

ARCHIPPUS and LÝSIS of TARENTUM: middle of fifth century.
OPSIMUS of RHÊGIUM: contemporary, or a generation later.
Pythagoreans; no writings survive. Lysis was sometimes credited with having written books ascribed to Pythagoras.

47. ARCHÝTAS OF TARENTUM

ARCHÝTAS of TARENTUM: first half of fourth century B.C.
Wrote in literary Doric a work on *Mathematical Science*, and on *Harmony*; possibly also one on *Mechanics*.

1. Mathematicians seem to me to have excellent discernment, and it is in no way strange that they should think correctly concerning the nature of particular existences. For since they have passed an excellent judgement on the nature of the Whole, they were bound to have an excellent view of separate things. Indeed, they have handed on to us a clear judgement on the speed of the constellations and their rising and setting, as well as on (*plane*) geometry and Numbers (*arithmetic*) and solid geometry, and not least on music; for these mathematical studies appear to be related. For they are concerned with things that are related, namely the two primary forms of Being.

First of all therefore, mathematicians have judged that sound is impossible unless there occurs a striking of objects against one another. This striking, they said, occurs when moving objects meet one another and collide. Now things moving in opposite directions, when they meet, produce a sound by simultaneously relaxing (*i.e. checking each · other's speed*). But things moving in the same direction though at unequal speeds create a sound by being struck when overtaken by what is following behind. Now many of these sounds cannot be recognised by our nature, some because of the faintness of the sound, others because of their great distance from us, and some even because of their excessive loudness,

78

for the big sounds cannot make their way into our hearing — just as, in vessels with narrow necks, when one pours in too much, nothing enters. Thus when things impinge on the perception, those which reach us quickly and powerfully from the source of sound seem high-pitched, while those which reach us slowly and feebly seem low-pitched. For if one takes a rod and strikes an object slowly and feebly, he will produce a low note with the blow, but if he strikes quickly and powerfully, a high note. Moreover, we can know (*this*) not only by this means, but also because when in speaking or singing we wish to produce a loud high sound, we employ strong exhalation as we utter . . .

This happens also with missiles. Those which are vigorously thrown are carried far, those weakly thrown (*fall*) near; for the air yields more readily before those which are vigorously thrown, whereas it yields less readily to those which are weakly thrown. This is bound to happen also with the notes of the voice: if a note is expelled by a forcible breath, it will be loud and high, if by a feeble breath, soft and low. But we can also see it from this, the strongest piece of evidence, namely, that when a man shouts loudly, we can hear him from a distance, whereas if the same man speaks softly, we cannot hear him even near at hand. Further, in flutes, when the breath expelled from the mouth falls on the holes nearest the mouth, a higher note is given out because of the greater force, but when it falls on the holes further away, a lower note results. Clearly swift motion produces a high-pitched sound, slow motion a low-pitched sound.

Moreover, the 'whirlers'[1] which are swung round at the Mysteries: if they are whirled gently, they give out a low note, if vigorously, a high note. So too with the reed: if one stops its lower end and blows, it gives out a low kind of note; but if one blows into the middle or some part of it, it will sound high; for the same breath passes weakly through the long distance, powerfully through the lesser.

That high notes are in swift motion, low notes in slow motion, has become clear to us from many examples.

2. There are three 'means' in music: one is the arithmetic, the second is the geometric, and the third is the subcontrary,

---

[1] ρόμβος, an instrument whirled round on a string at the Mysteries.

which they call 'harmonic'. The arithmetic mean is when there are three terms showing successively the same excess: the second exceeds the third by the same amount as the first exceeds the second. In this proportion, the ratio of the larger numbers is less, that of the smaller numbers greater.[1] The geometric mean is when the second is to the third as the first is to the second; in this, the greater numbers have the same ratio as the smaller numbers.[2] The subcontrary, which we call harmonic, is as follows: by whatever part of itself the first term exceeds the second, the middle term exceeds the third by the same part of the third. In this proportion, the ratio of the larger numbers is larger, and of the lower numbers less.[3]

3. In subjects of which one has no knowledge, one must obtain knowledge either by learning from someone else, or by discovering it for oneself. That which is learnt, therefore, comes from another and by outside help; that which is discovered comes by one's own efforts and independently. To discover without seeking is difficult and rare, but if one seeks, it is frequent and easy; if, however, one does not know how to seek, discovery is impossible.

Right Reckoning, when discovered, checks civil strife and increases concord; for where it has been achieved, there can be no excess of gain, and equality reigns. It is this (*Right Reckoning*) that brings us to terms over business contracts, and through it the poor receive from the men of means, and the rich give to the needy, both trusting that through it (*Right Reckoning*) they will be treated fairly. Being the standard and the deterrent of wrongdoers, it checks those who are able to reckon (*consequences*) before they do wrong, convincing them that they will not be able to avoid detection when they come against it; but when they are not able (*to reckon*) it shows them that in this[4] lies their wrongdoing, and so it prevents them from committing the wrong deed.

(*Attributed to a work entitled 'Conversations'*)

4. Arithmetic, it seems, in regard to wisdom is far superior to all the other sciences, especially geometry, because arith-

---

[1] *e.g.*, 6, 4, 2; $6 - 4 = 4 - 2$, and $\frac{6}{4} < \frac{4}{2}$

[2] *e.g.*, 8, 4, 2; $2:4 = 4:2$, and $\frac{4}{2} = \frac{8}{4}$

[3] *e.g.*, 6, 4, 3; $6 - 4 = 2$, $4 - 3 = 1$, and $2:6 = 1:3$; $\frac{6}{4} > \frac{4}{3}$

[4] *i.e.*, in their inability to reckon consequences (Kranz).

metic is able to treat more clearly any problem it will . . . and — a thing in which geometry fails — arithmetic adds proofs, and at the same time, if the problem concerns 'forms' (*i.e. numerical first principles*), arithmetic treats of the forms also.

(*Doubtful titles attributed to Archytas*)
5-8. 'On the Decad.' 'On Nature.' 'On Flutes.' 'On Mechanics.' 'On Agriculture.'

9. (*List of spurious titles*).

48. OCCELUS (OR OCELLUS) OF LUCANIA

OCCELUS (or OCELLUS) of LUCANIA: date uncertain.

Titles of several works were ascribed to him; but passages from a treatise *On the Nature of the Whole* are thought to be a forgery.

49. TÎMAEUS OF ITALIAN LOCRI

TÎMAEUS of ITALIAN LOCRI.

Nothing is known of him except from Plato's dialogue. A treatise *On the Soul of the Universe and Nature* ascribed to him is a forgery derived from Plato's *Timaeus*.

50. HICETAS OF SYRACUSE

HICETAS of SYRACUSE: date unknown.

A Pythagorean; no writings are known.

51. ECPHANTUS OF SYRACUSE

ECPHANTUS of SYRACUSE: date uncertain.

A Pythagorean; no writings are known.

52. XENOPHILUS OF CHALCIDICÊ

XENOPHILUS of CHALCIDICÊ: first half of fourth century.

A Pythagorean; no writings are known.

53. DIOCLES, ECHECRATES, POLYMNASTUS, PHANTÔN, ARÎÔN OF PHLIÛS

DIOCLES, ECHECRATES, POLYMNASTUS, PHANTÔN, ARÎÔN of PHLIÛS: beginning of fourth century.

They formed a Pythagorean 'cell' at Phlius; no writings are known.

54. PRŌRUS OF CYRÊNÊ, AMŶCLAS, CLEINIAS OF TARENTUM

Prōrus of Cyrênê, Amŷclas, Cleinias of Tarentum.

Latter-day Pythagoreans; forged writings in the name of Prōrus and Cleinias were in circulation in later times, but no genuine writings survive.

55. DAMŌN AND PHINTIAS OF SYRACUSE

Damōn and Phintias of Syracuse.

Pythagoreans, living at Syracuse in the reign of Dionysius the Younger (367-56 b.c.). No writings are known.

56. SĪMUS OF POSEIDŌNIA; MYŌNIDES AND EUPHRANŌR

Sĩmus of Poseidōnia: fourth century.
Myōnides and Euphranōr.

Pythagoreans. No writings are known. Simus was accused of publishing certain Pythagorean discoveries as his own.

57. LYCŌN (OR LYCUS) OF TARENTUM

Lycōn (or Lycus) of Tarentum: late fourth century.

Wrote on the Pythagorean life; no extracts survive.

58. PYTHAGOREAN SCHOOL

Pythagorean School.

Accounts of Pythagoreanism derive mostly from Aristotle and the Peripatetic School (Aristoxenus, Theophrastus, Eudemus), and from the Neo-Platonists (Porphyry, Iamblichus, Proclus, Simplicius); there are also extracts and references in the compilers (Diogenes Laertius, Stobaeus) and the lexicographers. But these accounts are usually referred to the Pythagorean School in general, not to any particular member. It was a rule that discoveries were referred to Pythagoras himself; and Pythagoras left no writings.

59. ANAXAGORAS OF CLAZOMENAE

Anaxagoras of Clazomenae was in his prime about 460 b.c.

He wrote one book, which was on sale at Athens for one drachma at the end of the fifth century.

1. (*Opening sentences from his book 'On Natural Science'*): All Things[1] were together, infinite in number and in smallness. For the Small also was infinite. And since all were together, nothing was distinguishable because of its smallness. For Air and Aether dominated all things, both of them being infinite. For these are the most important (*Elements*) in the total mixture, both in number and in size.

2. Air and Aether are separated off from the surrounding multiplicity, and that which surrounds is infinite in number.

3. For in Small there is no Least, but only a Lesser: for it is impossible that Being should Not-Be;[2] and in Great there is always a Greater. And it is equal in number to the small, but each thing is to itself both great and small.

4. Conditions being thus, one must believe that there are many things of all sorts in all composite products; and the seeds of all Things, which contain all kinds of shapes and colours and pleasant savours. And men too were fitted together, and all other creatures which have life. And the men possessed both inhabited cities and artificial works just like ourselves, and they had sun and moon and the rest, just as we have, and the earth produced for them many and diverse things, of which they collected the most useful, and now use them for their dwellings. This I say concerning Separation, that it must have taken place not only with us, but elsewhere.

Before these things were separated off, all things were together, nor was any colour distinguishable, for the mixing of all Things prevented this, (*namely*) the mixing of moist and dry and hot and cold and bright and dark, and there was a great quantity of earth in the mixture, and seeds infinite in number, not at all like one another. For none of the other things either is like any other. And as this was so, one must believe that all Things were present in the Whole.

5. These things being thus separated off, one must understand that all things are in no wise less or more (for it is not possible for them to be more than All), but all things are forever equal (*in quantity*).

---

[1] Where χρήματα is used, 'Things' is spelt with a capital. See *Companion*, pp. 266-7.

[2] τὸ μή was emended by Zeller to τομῇ, which Burnet accepts: 'it cannot be that what is should cease to be by being cut'.

6.   And since there are equal (*quantitative*) parts of Great and Small, so too similarly in everything there must be everything. It is not possible (*for them*) to exist apart, but all things contain a portion of everything. Since it is not possible for the Least to exist, it cannot be isolated, nor come into being by itself; but as it was in the beginning, so now, all things are together. In all things there are many things, and of the things separated off, there are equal numbers in (*the categories*) Great and Small.

7.   So that the number of the things separated off cannot be known either in thought or in fact.

8.   The things in the one Cosmos are not separated off from one another with an axe, neither the Hot from the Cold, nor the Cold from the Hot.

9.   Thus these things circulate and are separated off by force and speed. The speed makes the force. Their speed is not like the speed of any of the Things now existing among mankind, but altogether many times as fast.

10.   How can hair come from not-hair, and flesh from not-flesh?

11.   In everything there is a portion of everything except Mind; and some things contain Mind also.

12.   Other things all contain a part of everything, but Mind is infinite and self-ruling, and is mixed with no Thing, but is alone by itself. If it were not by itself, but were mixed with anything else, it would have had a share of all Things, if it were mixed with anything; for in everything there is a portion of everything, as I have said before. And the things mixed (*with Mind*) would have prevented it, so that it could not rule over any Thing in the same way as it can being alone by itself. For it is the finest of all Things, and the purest, and has complete understanding of everything, and has the greatest power. All things which have life, both the greater and the less, are ruled by Mind. Mind took command of the universal revolution, so as to make (*things*) revolve at the outset. And at first things began to revolve from some small point, but now the revolution extends over a greater area, and will spread even further. And the things which were mixed together, and separated off, and divided, were all understood by Mind. And

whatever they were going to be, and whatever things were then in existence that are not now, and all things that now exist and whatever shall exist — all were arranged by Mind, as also the revolution now followed by the stars, the sun and moon, and the Air and Aether which were separated off. It was this revolution which caused the separation off. And dense separates from rare, and hot from cold, and bright from dark, and dry from wet. There are many portions of many things. And nothing is absolutely separated off or divided the one from the other except Mind. Mind is all alike, both the greater and the less. But nothing else is like anything else, but each individual thing is and was most obviously that of which it contains the most.

13. And when Mind began the motion, there was a separating-off[1] from all that was being moved; and all that Mind set in motion was separated (*internally*); and as things were moving and separating off (*internally*), the revolution greatly increased this (*internal*) separation.

14. Mind, which ever Is, certainly still exists also where all other things are, (*namely*) in the multiple surrounding (*mass*) and in the things which were separated off before, and in the things already separated off.

15. The dense and moist and cold and dark (*Elements*) collected here, where now is Earth, and the rare and hot and dry went outwards to the furthest part of the Aether.

16. From these, while they are separating off, Earth solidifies; for from the clouds, water is separated off, and from the water, earth, and from the earth, stones are solidified by the cold; and these rush outward rather than the water.

17. The Greeks have an incorrect belief on Coming into Being and Passing Away. No Thing comes into being or passes away, but it is mixed together or separated from existing Things. Thus they would be correct if they called coming into being 'mixing', and passing away 'separation-off'.

---

[1] I follow Burnet in taking ἀπεκρίνετο as impersonal; Diels-Kranz make Nous the subject, and translate: 'Mind severed itself from the moving Whole.' But the reference is to three events: the starting of the revolution by Mind; the separation of a portion from the Whole; and the internal sifting under the revolution.

18.   It is the sun that endows the moon with its brilliance.

19.   We give the name Iris to the reflection of the sun on the clouds. It is therefore the sign of a storm, for the water which flows round the cloud produces wind or forces out rain.

20.   (*Translation, purporting to be from Galen's commentary on Hippocrates, into Arabic and then Hebrew. But it is uncertain if the author quoted in the passage, called 'Ansaros' in Hebrew, is Anaxagoras; some have thought that the material is from Hesiod. It deals principally with the rising and setting of the Pleiads and the seasonal work connected with this period*).

21.   Through the weakness of the sense-perceptions, we cannot judge truth.

21a.   Visible existences are a sight of the unseen (*i.e. the present gives a view of the future*).

21b.   (*We are inferior to the animals in strength and swiftness*) but we have experience, memory and wisdom and skill for our use alone (*and so can collect their products*).

22.   Bird's milk (*used to mean 'white of egg'*).

Spurious
23.   (*From a Graeco-Syrian MS.: Praise of death, at any age*).

60. ARCHELÃUS OF ATHENS

ARCHELÃUS of ATHENS was in his prime about 450 B.C.
   He is credited with a prose work called *Physiologia*, and an elegiac poem of condolence for Cimon.

1.   (*Reference by Plutarch to his Elegies written for Cimon on the death of his wife Isodicê*).

1a.   The cold is a bond.

61. MÊTRODÕRUS OF LAMPSACUS

MÊTRODÕRUS of LAMPSACUS: second half of the fifth century B.C.
   Applied physical theories to the interpretation of Homer. No writings survive.

62. CLEIDÊMUS

CLEIDÊMUS: birthplace not known. Was active in the fifth century B.C.
No writings survive. He is credited by Aristotle and Theophrastus with various scientific speculations.

63. ÎDAEUS OF HÎMERA

ÎDAEUS of HÎMERA. Date unknown: he is thought to have been a contemporary of Anaxagoras.
Meteorologist. No writings survive.

64. DIOGENES OF APOLLÔNIA

DIOGENES of APOLLÔNIA (probably on the Black Sea), lived in the latter half of the fifth century B.C.

His longest surviving work was that *On Natural Science*; he also wrote, and mentioned in his main work, separate treatises on Meteorology, and On the Nature of Man; and an attack on the Natural Scientists, whom he called Sophists.

1. In starting any thesis, it seems to me, one should put forward as one's point of departure something incontrovertible; the expression should be simple and dignified.

2. It seems to me, to sum up the whole matter, that all existing things are created by the alteration of the same thing, and are the same thing. This is very obvious. For if the things now existing in this universe — earth and water and air and fire and all the other things which are seen to exist in this world: if any one of these were different in its own (*essential*) nature, and were not the same thing which was transformed in many ways and changed, in no way could things mix with one another, nor could there be any profit or damage which accrued from one thing to another, nor could any plant grow out of the earth, nor any animal or any other thing come into being, unless it were so compounded as to be the same. But all these things come into being in different forms at different times by changes of the same (*substance*), and they return to the same.

3. Such a distribution would not have been possible without Intelligence, (*namely*) that all things should have their measure:

87

winter and summer and night and day and rains and winds and periods of fine weather; other things also, if one will study them closely, will be found to have the best possible arrangement.

4. Further, in addition to these, there are also the following important indications: men and all other animals live by means of Air, which they breathe in, and this for them is both Soul (Life) and Intelligence, as had been clearly demonstrated in this treatise; and if this is taken from (*them*), Intelligence also leaves them.

5. And it seems to me that that which has Intelligence is that which is called Air by mankind; and further, that by this, all creatures are guided, and that it rules everything; for this in itself seems to me to be God and to reach everywhere and to arrange everything and to be in everything. And there is nothing which has no share of it; but the share of each thing is not the same as that of any other, but on the contrary there are many forms both of the Air itself and of Intelligence; for it is manifold in form: hotter and colder and dryer and wetter and more stationary or having a swifter motion; and there are many other differences inherent in it and infinite (*forms*) of savour and colour. Also in all animals the Soul is the same thing, (*namely*) Air, warmer than that outside in which we are, but much colder than that nearer the sun. This degree of warmth is not the same in any of the animals (and indeed, it is not the same among different human beings), but it differs, not greatly, but so as to be similar. But in fact, no one thing among things subject to change can possibly be exactly like any other thing, without becoming the same thing. Since therefore change is manifold, animals also are manifold and many, and not like one another either in form or in way of life or in intelligence, because of the large number of (*the results of*) changes. Nevertheless, all things live, see and hear by the same thing (*Air*), and all have the rest of Intelligence also from the same.

6. The blood-vessels in man are as follows: there are two main blood-vessels; these extend from the abdomen along the spinal column, one to the right, one to the left, going (*down*) to each of the legs correspondingly, and up to the head past the collar-bone through the throat. From these, blood-vessels

extend throughout the whole body: from the right-hand one to the right side, from the left-hand one to the left side; the two biggest to the heart along the spine, and others a little higher through the chest below the armpit to each of the corresponding arms. And the one is called splenetic (*after the spleen*), the other (*after the liver*) hepatic. The extreme end of each of them divides, one branch going to the thumb, the other to the wrist, and from these go fine and many-branched veins to the rest of the hand and the fingers. (*Two*) other finer blood-vessels lead from the original (*main*) blood-vessels on the right to the liver, and on the left to the spleen and the kidneys. Those extending to the legs divide at the point of attachment (*to the body*) and extend throughout the thigh; the largest of them goes behind the thigh and is thick where it emerges; a second goes inside the thigh and is a little less thick. Then they travel past the knee to the shin and the foot, as in the hands; and they descend into the ankle and thence to the toes.

From the chief blood-vessels, many fine veins divide off also to the abdomen and the sides. Those which extend to the head through the throat come into view as large blood-vessels in the neck; and from each of these, at its extremity, many divide off to the head, those on the right going to the left, those on the left going to the right; and they each end at the ear.

There is another blood-vessel on each side of the neck parallel to the large one, a little smaller than the latter; into this the majority of those from the head itself unite. These extend through the throat inside, and from each of them (*blood-vessels*) travel below the shoulder-blade and to the arms. And beside the splenetic and hepatic blood-vessels others a little smaller appear: these are opened when there is any pain under the skin, but if the pain is in the abdomen, the hepatic and splenetic vessels are bled. There are others also leading from these below the breasts. There are other fine ones again which lead from each (*of the main vessels*) through the spinal marrow to the testicles in men, and in women to the womb. (The main blood-vessels, which come from the abdomen, are broader, and then become finer, until they change over from right to left and from left to right). These are called after the semen. The thickest blood is swallowed up by the fleshy parts; but if any is left over after passing through these parts, it becomes fine and warm and foamlike.

7. And this (*Element*) itself is a body both everlasting and immortal; whereas of other things, some come into being and others pass away.

8. But this seems to me to be clear, that it is great and strong, everlasting and immortal and manifold in form.

9. (GALEN, *quoting* Rufus of Ephesus: *All medical men agree that the male foetus is formed sooner and moves sooner than the female; Diogenes alone says the contrary*).

10. (*Contracted form of the word 'full'*).

65. CRATYLUS OF ATHENS

CRATYLUS of ATHENS: latter half of fifth century B.C.
A Heracleitean. No writings survive.

66. ANTISTHENES OF EPHESUS

ANTISTHENES of EPHESUS: date not recorded.
A Heracleitean. No writings survive.

67. LEUCIPPUS OF ABDÊRA

LEUCIPPUS of ABDÊRA was in his prime about 430 B.C.
He was credited with one book, called *The Great World-Order*; and perhaps a monograph *On Mind*.

1. (*Title of book:* The Great World-Order, *here attributed to Democritus*).

1a. (*Restoration of Herculanean Papyrus in which Democritus is accused of plagiarising from 'The Great World-Order' of Leucippus*).
Certain terms of the Atomic Theory can probably be traced to Leucippus, e.g.
    Atoms ('uncuttables').
    Close-pressed (*units*).
    Great Void.
    Absection.
    Rhythm (*meaning 'form'*).

Contact (*meaning 'arrangement'*).
Aspect (*meaning 'position'*).
Entanglement.
Eddy.

2.   (*From a treatise 'On Mind'*). Nothing happens at random; everything happens out of reason and by necessity.

68. DÊMOCRITUS OF ABDERA

DÊMOCRITUS of ABDÊRA was in his prime about 420 B.C.

A large body of written work was produced at Abdera, during and after Democritus' time. Thrasyllus, Roman scholar of the first century A.D., using the work of Alexandrian scholars, arranged these works in tetralogies, according to their subject-matter. Ethics (Tetralogies I and II); Natural Science (III to VI); Mathematics (VII to IX); Music (X and XI); and Technical Works (XII and XIII). There were also a group of treatises under the title *Causes*; a group of monographs on various subjects, the genuineness of which is suspect; a large number of Maxims; and a group of forged writings on magic.

The TETRALOGIES OF THRASYLLUS

TETRALOGIES I and II: ETHICS.

oa.   (*Title*): '*Pythagoras.*'

ob.   (*Title*): '*On the Character of the Sage.*'

oc.   (*Title*): '*On those in Hades.*'

1.   (*Title*): '*On Hades.*'

1a.   (*On making a will: those who cannot endure to do so*) are compelled to endure a double lot (*? die twice*).

1b.   (*Title*): '*Tritogeneia*' (*taken to mean 'three-fold in origin', on the Threeness of things*).

2.   (*Title*): '*Tritogeneia*', *of the three-fold character of Athene as Wisdom*.

2a.   (*Title*): '*On Courage.*'

2b.   (*Title*): '*The Horn of Amaltheia.*'

2c.   (*Title*): '*On Cheerfulness or Well-Being.*'

3. The man who wishes to have serenity of spirit should not engage in many activities, either private or public, nor choose activities beyond his power and natural capacity. He must guard against this, so that when good fortune strikes him and leads him on to excess by means of (*false*) seeming, he must rate it low, and not attempt things beyond his powers. A reasonable fullness is better than overfullness.

4. Pleasure and absence of pleasure are the criteria of what is profitable and what is not.

4a. (*Title*): 'Ethical Notes.'

TETRALOGIES III to VI: NATURAL SCIENCE, INCLUDING LOGIC

4b. (*Title*): 'Great World-Order' (*usually ascribed to Leucippus*). *Democritus is said to have plagiarised it in his* 'Small World-Order'.

4c. (*Title*): 'Small World-Order'.

5. (*In the* 'Small World-Order', *Democritus said he was*) a young man in the old age of Anaxagoras. (*He said he wrote the book* 730 *years after the fall of Troy, and that Anaxagoras' views on the sun were not original but ancient, and he ridiculed his views on the arrangement of the universe and on Mind*).

Titles

5a. 'On Cosmography.'

5b. 'On the Planets.'

5c. 'On Nature' or 'On the Nature of the Universe'.

5d. 'On Nature' (*Second Part*), or 'On the Nature of Man', or 'On Flesh'.

5e. 'On Mind.'

5f. 'On Perception.'

5g. 'On Tastes.'

5h. 'On Colours.'

5i. 'On the Different Forms.'

6. One must learn by this rule that Man is severed from reality. (*From* 'On the Forms'.)

7. We know nothing about anything really, but Opinion is for all individuals an inflowing (*? of the Atoms*). (*From 'On the Forms'.*)

8. It will be obvious that it is impossible to understand how in reality each thing is. (*From 'On the Forms'.*)

8a. (*Title*): '*On Changes of Form.*'

8b. (*Title*): '*On Strengthening Arguments.*'

9. Sweet exists by convention, bitter by convention, colour by convention; atoms and Void (*alone*) exist in reality ... We know nothing accurately in reality, but (*only*) as it changes according to the bodily condition, and the constitution of those things that flow upon (*the body*) and impinge upon it.

10. It has often been demonstrated that we do not grasp how each thing is or is not.

10a. (*Title*): '*On Images*' or '*On Foresight*'. (*?*)

10b. (*Title*): '*On Logic*' or '*The Canon*'. (*3 Books*).

11. There are two sorts of knowledge, one genuine, one bastard (*or 'obscure'*). To the former belong all the following: sight, hearing, smell, taste, touch. The real is separated from this. When the bastard can do no more — neither see more minutely, nor hear, nor smell, nor taste, nor perceive by touch — and a finer investigation is needed, then the genuine comes in as having a tool for distinguishing more finely. (*From 'The Canon'*).

11a. (*Title*): '*On Difficult Problems.*'

UNCLASSIFIED WRITINGS ON 'CAUSES'

(*Titles*)
11b. '*Heavenly Causes.*'

11c. '*Aerial Causes.*'

11d. '*Surface Causes.*'

11e. '*Causes of Fire and Things in Fire.*'

11f. '*Causes of Sounds.*'

11g. 'Causes of Seeds, Plants and Fruits.'

11h. 'Causes of Animals.' (3 Books).

11i. 'Mixed Causes.'

11k. 'On the Magnet.'

TETRALOGIES VII to IX: MATHEMATICAL

(Titles)
11l. 'On Difference of Comprehension'[1] or, 'On the Contact of Circle and Sphere'.

11m. 'On Geometry.'

11n. 'On Geometrical Problems.'

11o. 'Numbers.'

11p. 'On Disproportionate Lines and Solids.'

11q. 'Projections.'

11r. 'The Great Year', or, 'Astronomy'. 'Calendar.'

12. (The Great Year of Philolaus and Democritus is of 82 years with 28 intercalary months).

13. (Use of contracted form of 'mine').

14. (Remains of Astronomical Calendar).

1. (VITRUVIUS). Following the discoveries of the natural philosophers (Thales, Anaxagoras, Pythagoras, Xenophanes, Democritus) others invented the method of Parapêgmata,[2] showing the rising and setting of the constellations, and the signs of storms, namely, Eudoxus, Euctemon, Callippus, Meton, Philippus, Hipparchus, Aratus and others.

2. (EUDOXUS). Winter solstice on the 19th or 20th. From the autumn equinox to the winter solstice, 91 days. From the winter solstice to the spring equinox, 19 days.

[1] Some emend γνώμης to γνώμονος ('Gnômôn'); Heath prefers γωνίης ('angle'). See Greek Mathematics, I, p. 178.
[2] Diels: 'The Parapêgma was a bronze or marble indicator of the days of the solar year according to the Zodiac, together with the customary weather-signs. Beside the days were holes in which the days of the civil month could be inserted.'

94

3. (*Calendar of 2nd century B.C. attributed to* GEMINUS, *containing extracts from Democritus' Calendar*).

Scorpio: 4th day. Pleiades set at dawn. Wintry winds, cold and frost as
            a rule. Leaves begin to fall.
            13th. Lyra rises at dawn. Winter weather.
Sagittarius: 16th. Aëtos rises. Thunder and lightning. Rain or wind or
            both.
Capricorn: 12th. South wind.
Aquarius: 3rd. Storm. Unlucky day.
            16th. Zephyr begins to blow and remains. 43 days from the
            Solstice.
Pisces: 4th. Halcyon days.
            14th. The Bird-winds (cold) blow and last 9 days.
Ram: Pleiades set at sunrise and remain invisible for 40 nights.
Twins: 10th. Rain.
            29th. Orion rises.

4. (PLINY). *The winter will be like the winter solstice and
the three days before and after it; and similarly the summer
like the summer solstice. Dates of rising of Capella and the
Kids: 28th and 29th September. (Democritus agrees in this
with Philippus and Eudoxus, which is rare).*

5. (SCHOLIAST on Apollonius Rhodius). *On the rising of
Arcturus there is violent rain.*

6. (CLODIUS' Calendar in Joannes Lydus). *Democritus
was the first to give certain meteorological information.*

7. (PTOLEMAEUS). *Weather signs observed by Democritus
in Northern Greece. He said that the most important day was
the fifteenth day after the equinox.*

Sept. 14 Swallow leaves.   (Change of weather).
      26 Rain and wind-disturbances.
Oct.   5 Storm. Sowing-time.
      29 Cold or frost.
Nov. 13 Storm on land and sea.
      27 Disturbed sky and sea.
Dec.   5 Storm.
      10 Thunder, lightning, rain, wind.
      27 Very stormy.
      29 Change of weather.
Jan.   4 South wind as a rule.
      20 Rain.
      24 Great storm.
Feb.   6 West wind begins.
       8 West wind blows.
      24 The days called halcyon.

Mar. 7   Cold winds. Bird-days (nine).[1]

18   Change of weather, Cold wind.

27   Change of weather.

Apr. 24   Change of weather.

May 28   Rain.

June 3   Rain.

22   Good day.

28   West wind, morning rain, then strong north winds for 7 days.

July 16   Rain. Squalls.

26   South wind and heat.

Aug. 19   Change of weather, with rain and wind.

8. (JOANNES LYDUS' Calendar).

Jan. 15   South-west wind with rain.

18   Dolphin sets; Change of weather usually.

23   South-west wind blows.

Mar. 17   Setting of Pisces, *on the day of the Bacchanalia.*

Sept. 2   Change of wind, and prevalence of rain.

Oct. 6   Rise of Kids; north wind blows.

Nov. 25   The Sun in Sagittarius.

(End of Extracts from Calendar)

(Titles)

14a.   *'Contest according to the Water-Clock'* (?)

14b.   *'Description of the Heavens.'*

14c.   *'Description of the Earth.'*

15.   *'Voyage round the World.'* (AGATHÊMERUS: *After Anaximander, descriptions of a Voyage Round the World were written by Hecataeus, Hellanicus, and Damastes of Sigeion copying for the most part Hellanicus. Democritus and Eudoxus followed, and some others. The ancients described the world as round, with Greece in the centre, and Delphi the centre of Greece. But Democritus, a man of wide experience, was the first to describe it as rectängular, the length half the width. Dicaearchus the Peripatetic concurred*).

15a.   *'Description of the Pole.'*

15b.   *'Description of Rays.'*

TETRALOGIES X and XI: MUSIC

15c.   *(Title)*: *'On Rhythm and Harmony'*.

16.   *(Musaeus invented the dactylic hexameter).*

[1] Bird-days are those on which migrant birds appear; bird-winds are those which bring migrant birds.

16a. (*Title*): '*On Poetry.*'

17. (*There is no poetry without madness*).

18. What a poet writes with enthusiasm and divine inspiration is most beautiful.

18a. (*Title*): '*On the Beauty of Words.*'

18b. (*Title*): '*On well-sounding and ill-sounding Letters.*'

19. (EUSTATHIUS: *Democritus, like all Ionians, calls the letter Gamma 'Gemma'; he also calls the letter Mu 'Mô'*.

20. (SCHOLIAST on Dionysius Thrax: *The names of the letters are indeclinable; but Democritus declines them*).

20a. (*Title*): '*On Homer, or a Correct Diction and Vocabulary.*'

21. Homer, having been gifted with a divine nature, built an ordered structure of manifold verse.

22. The eagle has black bones.

23. (SCHOLIAST on Homer: *The Trojan herald speaking to the Greeks says of Paris 'Would that he had perished first!*' ('*Iliad,*' VII. 390). *Democritus thinks that he spoke this as an aside, because it would not be proper for him to say this in front of all the Greeks*).

24. (EUSTATHIUS on Homer, *Od.*, XV. 374: *The loyal slave Eumaeus was so highly regarded by the ancients that they even provide him with a mother: Democritus says she was Poverty*).

25. (EUSTATHIUS on Homer, *Od.*, XII. 62: *Some think that the Sun is Zeus, others, with Democritus, that the vapour on which the sun feeds is ambrosia*).

25a. (*Title*): '*On Song.*'

25b. (*Title*): '*On Phrases.*'

26. (PROCLUS: *Pythagoras and Epicurus agree with Cratylus, but Democritus and Aristotle agree with Hermogenes, the former that names arise by nature, the latter that they arise by chance. Pythagoras thought that the Soul gave the names, deriving them like images of reality from the mind. But Democritus thought that the proof of their chance origin was fourfold:* (1) *the calling of different things by the same name;* (2) *having several names for the same thing;* (3) *change of name;* (4) *lack of name.*

97

26a.   (*Title*): '*On Nomenclature.*'

TETRALOGIES XII and XIII: ON MEDICAL TECHNIQUE, AGRI-
CULTURE, etc.

(*Titles*)
26b.   '*Prognosis.*'

26c.   '*On Diet.*'

26d.   '*On Medical Method.*'

26e.   '*Causes of Seasonable and Unseasonable Things.*'

26f.   '*On Farming.*'

27.   (COLUMELLA: *Democritus and Mago say that vine-yards
should face north for the best crops*).

27a.   (COLUMELLA: *Democritus and Mago say that bees can be
generated from a dead cow*).

28.   (COLUMELLA: *Democritus in his book 'On Farming' says that
it is foolish to encircle a garden with walls: if made of sun-dried
bricks, they cannot stand the weather; if of stone, they cost more than
they are worth; and to surround a large piece of land with a wall
demands a large inheritance*).

(*Titles*)
28a.   '*On Painting.*'

28b.   '*Tactics.*'[1]

28c.   '*Fighting in Armour.*'[1]
       (*End of the Tetralogies of Thrasyllus*)

GENUINE FRAGMENTS FROM UNSPECIFIED WORKS

29.   (*Democritus called the rim of the shield*) 'circuit'.

29a.   (*Democritus used contracted forms of the personal pronouns
'we, you, they*').

30.   Of the reasoning men, a few, raising their hands thither
to what we Greeks call the Air nowadays, said: 'Zeus considers
all things and he knows all and gives and takes away all and is
King of all.'

---

[1] These are thought to be the work of another Democritus, who according to
Suidas wrote two books on Tactics and one on the Jews: perhaps Democritus of Mendê.

31. Medicine heals diseases of the body, wisdom frees the soul from passions.

32. Coition is a slight attack of apoplexy. For man gushes forth from man, and is separated by being torn apart with a kind of blow.[1]

33. Nature and instruction are similar; for instruction transforms the man, and in transforming, creates his nature.

34. Man is a universe in little (*Microcosm*).

GNÔMAE[2]

35. If any man listens to my opinions, here recorded, with intelligence, he will achieve many things worthy of a good man, and avoid doing many unworthy things.

36. =187.

37. He who chooses the advantages of the soul chooses things more divine, but he who chooses those of the body, chooses things human.

38. It is noble to prevent the criminal; but if one cannot, one should not join him in crime.

39. One must either be good, or imitate a good man.

40. Men find happiness neither by means of the body nor through possessions, but through uprightness and wisdom.

41. Refrain from crimes not through fear but through duty.

42. It is a great thing, when one is in adversity, to think of duty.

43. Repentance for shameful deeds is salvation in life.

44. =225.

45. The wrongdoer is more unfortunate than the man wronged.

---

[1] Pun on ἀποπληξίη and πληγή.

[2] Given in a collection called 'Maxims of Democratês'. But Stobaeus quotes as 'Maxims of Democritus' many of the sayings here recorded; it is therefore thought that 'Democrates' is a corruption of 'Democritus', or perhaps a later attribution by Byzantine scholars who had discovered the existence of one Democrates of Aphidna in Attica, a writer on agriculture of the fourth century B.C.

46. Magnanimity consists in enduring tactlessness with mildness.

47. Well-ordered behaviour consists in obedience to the law, the ruler, and the man wiser (*than oneself*).

48. When inferior men censure, the good man pays no heed.

49. It is hard to be governed by one's inferior.

50. The man completely enslaved to wealth can never be honest.

51. In power of persuasion, reasoning is far stronger than gold.

52. He who tries to give intelligent advice to one who thinks he has intelligence, is wasting his time.

53. Many who have not learnt Reason, nevertheless live according to reason.

53a. Many whose actions are most disgraceful practise the best utterances.

54. The foolish learn sense through misfortune.

55. One should emulate the deeds and actions of virtue, not the words.

56. Noble deeds are recognised and emulated by those of natural good disposition.

57. Good breeding in cattle depends on physical health, but in men on a well-formed character.

58. The hopes of right-thinking men are attainable, but those of the unintelligent are impossible.

59. Neither skill nor wisdom is attainable unless one learns.

60. It is better to examine one's own faults than those of others.

61. Those whose character is well-ordered have also a well-ordered life.

62. Virtue consists, not in avoiding wrong-doing, but in having no wish thereto.

63. To pronounce praise on noble deeds is noble; for to do so over base deeds is the work of a false deceiver.

64. Many much-learned men have no intelligence.[1]

65. One should practise much-sense, not much-learning.[1]

66. It is better to deliberate before action than to repent afterwards.

67. Believe not everything, but only what is approved: the former is foolish, the latter the act of a sensible man.

68. The worthy and the unworthy man (*are to be known*) not only by their actions, but also their wishes.

69. For all men, good and true are the same; but pleasant differs for different men.

70. Immoderate desire is the mark of a child, not a man.

71. Untimely pleasures produce unpleasantnesses.

72. Violent desire for one thing blinds the soul to all others.

73. Virtuous love consists in decorous desire for the beautiful.

74. Accept no pleasure unless it is beneficial.

75. It is better for fools to be ruled than to rule.

76. For the foolish, not reason but advantage is the teacher.

77. Fame and wealth without intelligence are dangerous possessions.

78. To make money is not without use, but if it comes from wrong-doing, nothing is worse.

79. It is a bad thing to imitate the bad, and not even to wish to imitate the good.

80. It is shameful to be so busy over the affairs of others that one knows nothing of one's own.

81. Constant delay means work undone.

82. The false and the seeming-good are those who do all in word, not in fact.

[1] Cp. Heracleitus, Frg. 40.

83. The cause of error is ignorance of the better.

84. The man who does shameful deeds must first feel shame in his own eyes.

85. He who contradicts and chatters much is ill-fitted for learning what he ought.

86. It is greed to do all the talking and not be willing to listen.

87. One must be on one's guard against the bad man, lest he seize his opportunity.

88. The envious man torments himself like an enemy.

89. An enemy is not he who injures, but he who wishes to do so.

90. The enmity of relatives is much worse than that of strangers.

91. Be not suspicious towards all, but be cautious and firm.

92. Accept favours in the foreknowledge that you will have to give a greater return for them.

93. When you do a favour, study the recipient first, lest he prove a scoundrel and repay evil for good.

94. Small favours at the right time are greatest to the recipients.

95. Marks of honour are greatly valued by right-thinking men, who understand why they are being honoured.

96. The generous man is he who does not look for a return, but who does good from choice.

97. Many who seem friendly are not so, and those who do not seem so, are.

98. The friendship of one intelligent man is better than that of all the unintelligent.[1]

99. Life is not worth living for the man who has not even one good friend.

[1] Cp. Heracleitus, Frg. 49.

100. The man whose tested friends do not stay long with him is bad-tempered.

101. Many avoid their friends when they fall from wealth to poverty.

102. In all things, equality is fair, excess and deficiency not so, in my opinion.

103. The man who loves nobody is, I think, loved by no one.

104. In old age, a man is agreeable if his manner is pleasant and his speech serious.

105. Physical beauty is (*merely*) animal unless intelligence be present.

106. In prosperity it is easy to find a friend, in adversity nothing is so difficult.

107. Not all one's relatives are friends, but only those who agree with us about what is advantageous.

107a. It is proper, since we are human beings, not to laugh at the misfortunes of others, but to mourn.

108. Good things are obtained with difficulty if one seeks; but bad things come without our even seeking.

109. The censorious are not well-fitted for friendship.

110. A woman must not practise argument: this is dreadful.

111. To be ruled by a woman is the ultimate outrage for a man.

112. It is the mark of the divine intellect to be always calculating something noble.

113. Those who praise the unintelligent do (*them*) great harm.

114. It is better to be praised by another than by oneself.

115. If you do not recognise (*i.e. understand*) praise, believe that you are being flattered.

(*End of the Gnômae*)

116. I came to Athens and no one knew me.

117. We know nothing in reality; for truth lies in an abyss.

118. (*I would*) rather discover one cause than gain the kingdom of Persia.

119. Men have fashioned an image of Chance as an excuse for their own stupidity. For Chance rarely conflicts with Intelligence, and most things in life can be set in order by an intelligent sharpsightedness.

120. Pulse-beat (*word for*).

121. (*Unusual word*) Ownest.

122. Pitfalls (*word used by hunters*).

122a. (*Derivation of 'gynê', woman, from 'gonê', seed*).

123. (*Word for*) image (*as effluence from objects*).

124. (*Corrupt*) Men shall be one man, and a man shall be all men. (*Meaning unknown*).

125. Colour exists by convention (*usage*), sweet by convention, bitter by convention.
   (*Reply of the senses to Intellect*): 'Miserable Mind, you get your evidence from us, and do you try to overthrow us? The overthrow will be your downfall'.

126. (*All creatures*) which move along their path in a wave-like manner.

127. Men get pleasure from scratching themselves: they feel an enjoyment like that of lovemaking.

128-141. (*Unusual words quoted by grammarians*)

128. Straight-bored.

129. They think divine thoughts with their mind.

129a. Is leaned.

130. Circular bands.

131. Untrodden (*unevenly compounded*).

132. Equilateral.

133. Sodden.

134. Noose.

135. Receptacles (*of the blood-vessels*).

136. Covers with a lid.

137. Combination.

138. Change of arrangement.

139. Change of form.

139a. Change of colour.

140. Well-being (*for 'happiness'*).

141. Form (*for 'atom'*).

142. (*The names of the gods are*) vocal images (*i.e. express their nature*).

143. (*On anger*): All imaginable ills (*flow from it*).

144. (*Music is the youngest of the arts*) For it was not necessity that separated it off (*i.e. created it*), but it arose from the existing superfluity.

144a. I will return (*to the beginning*).

145. Speech is the shadow of action.

146. The Reason within the soul, accustoming itself to derive its pleasures from itself.

147. Pigs revel in mud.

148. The navel forms first in the womb, as an anchorage against tossing and wandering, a cable and a rope for the fruit, engendered and future.

149. (*Inside, we are*) a complex store-house and treasury of ills, with many possibilities of suffering.

150. (*One must eschew the arguments of*) wranglers and word-twisters.

151. In a shared fish, there are no bones.

152. There is no lightning sent from Zeus which does not contain the pure light of the Aether.

153. To please one's neighbours (*brings damage*).

154. We are pupils of the animals in the most important things: the spider for spinning and mending, the swallow for building, and the songsters, swan and nightingale, for singing, by way of imitation.

155. If a cone were cut by a plane parallel to the base,[1] what ought one to think of the surfaces resulting from the section: are they equal or unequal? If they are unequal, they will make the cone have many steplike indentations and unevennesses; but if they are equal, the sections will be equal, and the cone will appear to have the same property as a cylinder, being made up of equal, not unequal, circles, which is most absurd.

155a. (ARISTOTLE: *Democritus treats the sphere as a sort of angle when cutting it*).

156. Naught exists just as much as Aught.

157. Learn thoroughly the art of statesmanship, which is the greatest, and pursue its toils, from which men win great and brilliant prizes.

158. Men thinking new thoughts with each day.

159. (*Democritus said*): If the body brought a suit-against the soul, for all the pains it had endured throughout life, and the illtreatment, and I were to be the judge of the suit, I would gladly condemn the soul, in that it had partly ruined the body by its neglect and dissolved it with bouts of drunkenness, and partly destroyed it and torn it in pieces with its passion for pleasure — as if, when a tool or a vessel were in a bad condition, I blamed the man who was using it carelessly.

160. (*To live badly is*) not to live badly, but to spend a long time dying.

161. (SCHOLIAST on Apollonius Rhodius: *Eclipses were called 'down-drawings' up to the time of Democritus, with reference to the ancient belief that sorceresses could draw down the sun and moon and so cause eclipses*).

162. (SCHOLIAST on Homer, *Iliad*, XIII. 137: *Democritus uses the epic word for 'large boulder' for the cylinder*).

---

[1] 'By which is clearly meant a plane indefinitely near to the base.' Heath, *Greek Mathematics*, I, pp. 179-80.

163. (SEXTUS: *Democritus mentions Xeniades of Corinth*).

164. Living creatures consort with their kind, as doves with doves, and cranes with cranes, and similarly with the rest of the animal world. So it is with inanimate things, as one can see with the sieving of seeds and with the pebbles on beaches. In the former, through the circulation of the sieve, beans are separated and ranged with beans, barley-grains with barley, and wheat with wheat; in the latter, with the motion of the wave, oval pebbles are driven to the same place as oval, and round to round, as if the similarity in these things had a sort of power over them which had brought them together.

165. I say the following about the Whole ... Man is that which we all know.

166. (SEXTUS: *Democritus said that*) certain images visit men (*some beneficent, some harmful. He prayed*) to meet with fortunate images.

167. An eddy, of all manner of forms, is separated off from the Whole.

168. (SIMPLICIUS: *The Democriteans called the atoms 'nature'.* ... *For they said that these were*) scattered about.

169. Do not try to understand everything, lest you become ignorant of everything.

170. Happiness, like unhappiness, is a property of the soul.

171. Happiness does not dwell in flocks of cattle or in gold. The soul is the dwelling-place of the (*good and evil*) genius.

172. Those same things from which we get good can also be for us a source of hurt, or else we can avoid the hurt. For instance, deep water is useful for many purposes, and yet again harmful; for there is danger of being drowned. A technique has therefore been invented: instruction in swimming.

173. For mankind, evil comes out of what is good, if one does not know how to guide and drive correctly. It is not right to place such things in the category of evil, but in that of good. It is possible also to use what is good for an evil end[1] if one wishes.

---

[1] The MS. reading ἀλκήν is emended by Diels-Kranz to ἀλκῆ and translated: 'It is possible to use what is good as a help against what is evil.'

174. The cheerful man, who is impelled towards works that are just and lawful, rejoices by day and by night, and is strong and free from care. But the man who neglects justice, and does not do what he ought, finds all such things disagreeable when he remembers any of them, and he is afraid and torments himself.

175. But the gods are the givers of all good things, both in the past and now. They are not, however, the givers of things which are bad, harmful or non-beneficial, either in the past or now, but men themselves fall into these through blindness of mind and lack of sense.

176. Chance is generous but unreliable. Nature, however, is self-sufficient. Therefore it is victorious, by means of its smaller but reliable (*power*) over the greater promise of hope.

177. Neither can fine speech cover up base action, nor can good action be injured by calumny.

178. Worst of all things is frivolity as the educator of youth, for it breeds those pleasures from which wickedness comes.

179. If children are allowed not to work,[1] they cannot learn letters or music or gymnastic, nor that which above all things embraces virtue, (*namely*) reverence. For it is precisely from these studies that reverence usually grows.

180. Education is an ornament for the prosperous, a refuge for the unfortunate.

181. The man who employs exhortation and persuasion will turn out to be a more effective guide to virtue than he who employs law and compulsion. For the man who is prevented by law from wrongdoing will probably do wrong in secret, whereas the man who is led towards duty by persuasion will probably not do anything untoward either secretly or openly. Therefore the man who acts rightly through understanding and knowledge becomes at the same time brave and upright.

182. Beautiful objects are wrought by study through effort, but ugly things are reaped automatically without toil. For

[1] It seems best to take μὴ ποιεῖν, after the intrans. ἀνιέντες, as a consecutive infinitive: 'If children are left free so as not to work.' Kranz translates: 'If we do not leave children free to work.'

even one who is unwilling is sometimes so wrought upon by learning . . . . . (? *MSS. corrupt*).

183. There is an intelligence of the young, and an un-intelligence of the aged. It is not time that teaches wisdom, but early training and natural endowment.

184. Continuous association with base men increases a disposition to crime.

185. The hopes of the educated are better than the wealth of the ignorant.

186. Similarity of outlook creates friendship.

187. It is right that men should value the soul rather than the body; for perfection of soul corrects the inferiority of the body, but physical strength without intelligence does nothing to improve the mind.

188. The criterion of the advantageous and disadvantageous is enjoyment and lack of enjoyment.

189. The best way for a man to lead his life is to have been as cheerful as possible and to have suffered as little as possible. This could happen if one did not seek one's pleasures in mortal things.

190. One must avoid even speaking of evil deeds.

191. Cheerfulness is created for men through moderation of enjoyment and harmoniousness of life. Things that are in excess or lacking are apt to change and cause great disturbance in the soul. Souls which are stirred by great divergences are neither stable nor cheerful. Therefore one must keep one's mind on what is attainable, and be content with what one has, paying little heed to things envied and admired, and not dwelling on them in one's mind. Rather must you consider the lives of those in distress, reflecting on their intense sufferings, in order that your own possessions and condition may seem great and enviable, and you may, by ceasing to desire more, cease to suffer in your soul. For he who admires those who have, and who are called happy by other mortals, and who dwells on them in his mind every hour, is constantly compelled to undertake something new and to run the risk, through

his desire, of doing something irretrievable among those things which the laws prohibit. Hence one must not seek the latter, but must be content with the former, comparing one's own life with that of those in worse cases, and must consider oneself fortunate, reflecting on their sufferings, in being so much better off than they. If you keep to this way of thinking, you will live more serenely, and will expel those not-negligible curses in life, envy, jealousy and spite.

192.   It is easy to praise and blame what one should not, but both are the marks of a corrupt character.

193.   It is the business of intelligence to guard against a threatened injustice, but it is the mark of insensibility not to avenge it when it has happened.

194.   The great pleasures come from the contemplation of noble works.

195.   . . . Images conspicuous for their dress and ornament, empty of heart.

196.   Forgetfulness of one's own ills breeds boldness.

197.   Fools are shaped by the gifts of chance, but those who understand these things by the gifts of wisdom.

198.   The animal needing something knows how much it needs, the man does not.

199.   People are fools who hate life and yet wish to live through fear of Hades.

200.   People are fools who live without enjoyment of life.

201.   People are fools who yearn for long life without pleasure in long life.

202.   People are fools who yearn for what is absent, but neglect what they have even when it is more valuable than what has gone.

203.   Men who shun death pursue it.

204.   Fools cannot satisfy anyone in the whole of life.

205.   Fools long for life because they fear death.

206.   Fools want to live to be old because they fear death.

207. One should choose not every pleasure, but only that concerned with the beautiful.

208. The self-control of the father is the greatest example for the children.

209. For a self-sufficiency in food, there is never a 'short night'. (*i.e. those who have independence of means do not suffer from insomnia*).

210. A rich table is provided by luck, but a sufficient one by wisdom.

211. Moderation multiplies pleasures, and increases pleasure.

212. Sleep in the daytime signifies bodily trouble or aberration of mind or laziness or lack of training.

213. Courage minimises difficulties.

214. The brave man is not only he who overcomes the enemy, but he who is stronger than pleasures. Some men are masters of cities, but are enslaved to women.

215. The reward of justice is confidence of judgement and imperturbability, but the end of injustice is the fear of disaster.

216. Imperturbable wisdom is worth everything.

217. They alone are dear to the gods to whom crime is hateful.

218. Riches derived from evil activity make the disgrace more conspicuous.

219. The passion for wealth, unless limited by satisfaction, is far more painful than extreme poverty; for greater passions create greater needs.

220. Evil gains bring loss of virtue.

221. The hope of evil gains is the beginning of damage.

222. The excessive accumulation of wealth for one's children is an excuse for covetousness, which thus displays its peculiar nature.

223. The things needed by the body are available to all without toil and trouble. But the things which require toil

and trouble and which make life disagreeable are not desired by the body but by the ill-constitution of the mind.

224. The desire for more loses what one has, like the dog in Aesop.

225. One should tell the truth, not speak at length.

226. Freedom of speech is the sign of freedom; but the danger lies in discerning the right occasion.

227. Misers have the fate of bees: they work as if they were going to live for ever.

228. The children of misers, if they are reared in ignorance, are like those dancers who leap between swords: if they miss, in their leap downwards, a single place where they must plant their feet, they are destroyed. But it is hard to alight upon the one spot, because only the space for the feet is left. So too with the children of misers: if they miss the paternal character of carefulness and thrift, they are apt to be destroyed.

229. Thrift and fasting are beneficial; so too is expenditure at the right time. But to recognise this is the function of a good man.

230. The life without festival is a long road without an inn.

231. The right-minded man is he who is not grieved by what he has not, but enjoys what he has.

232. Of pleasures, those that come most rarely give the greatest enjoyment.

233. If one oversteps the due measure, the most pleasurable things become most unpleasant.

234. Men ask in their prayers for health from the gods, but do not know that the power to attain this lies in themselves; and by doing the opposite through lack of control, they themselves become the betrayers of their own health to their desires.

235. All who derive their pleasures from the stomach, overstepping due season in eating or drinking or sexual pleasure, have pleasures that are but brief and short-lived, (*that is*), only while they are eating and drinking, but pains that are many. For this desire is always present for the same things,

and when people get what they desire, the pleasure passes quickly, and they have nothing good for themselves except a brief enjoyment; and then again the need for the same things returns.

236. It is hard to fight desire; but to control it is the sign of a reasonable man.[1]

237. All bellicosity is foolish; for in studying the disadvantage of one's enemy, one loses sight of one's own advantage.

238. The man who strives against the stronger ends in disgrace.

239. Bad men, when they escape, do not keep the oaths which they make in time of stress.

240. Toils undertaken willingly make the endurance of those done unwillingly easier.

241. Continuous labour becomes easier through habit.

242. More men become good through practice than by nature.

243. All kinds of toil are pleasanter than rest, when men attain that for which they labour, or know that they will attain it. But whenever there is failure to attain, then labour is painful and hard.

244. Do not say or do what is base, even when you are alone. Learn to feel shame in your own eyes much more than before others.

245. The laws would not prevent each man from living according to his inclination, unless individuals harmed each other; for envy creates the beginning of strife.

246. Life in a foreign country teaches self-sufficiency; for bread and bed are the sweetest cures for hunger and fatigue.

247. To a wise man, the whole earth is open; for the native land of a good soul is the whole earth.

248. The law wishes to benefit men's life; and it is able to do so, when they themselves wish to receive benefit; for it shows to those who obey it their own particular virtue.

[1] Cp. Heracleitus, Frg. 85.

249. Civil war is harmful to both parties; for both to the conquerors and the conquered, the destruction is the same.

250. The greatest undertakings are carried through by means of concord, including wars between City-States: there is no other way.

251. Poverty under democracy is as much to be preferred to so-called prosperity under an autocracy as freedom to slavery.

252. One must give the highest importance to affairs of the State, that it may be well run; one must not pursue quarrels contrary to right, nor acquire a power contrary to the common good. The well-run State is the greatest protection, and contains all in itself; when this is safe, all is safe; when this is destroyed, all is destroyed.

253. To good men, it is not advantageous that they should neglect their own affairs for other things; for their private affairs suffer. But if a man neglects public affairs, he is ill spoken of, even if he steals nothing and does no wrong. And if he is[1] negligent and does wrong, he is liable not only to be ill-spoken of but also to suffer bodily harm. To make mistakes is inevitable, but men find it hard to forgive.

254. When base men enter upon office, the more unworthy they are, the more neglectful, and they are filled with folly and recklessness.

255. When the powerful prevail upon themselves to lend to the indigent, and help them, and benefit them, herein at last is pity, and an end to isolation, and friendship, and mutual aid, and harmony among the citizens; and other blessings such as no man could enumerate.

256. Justice is to do what should be done; injustice is to fail to do what should be done, and to put it aside.

257. With certain animals, the rule for killing them or not stands thus: any that do wrong and wish to do so may be killed with impunity, and it conduces to well-being to do so rather than not do so.

[1] Meineke inserted the negative μή, which was accepted by Diels-Kranz.

258. One must at all costs kill all those creatures which do hurt contrary to justice. The man who does this has the greater share of cheerfulness(?) and justice and courage and property(?) in every ordered society (*than he who does not*).[1]

259. As has been laid down (*by me*) regarding beasts and reptiles which are inimical (*to man*), so I think one should do with regard to human beings: one should, according to ancestral law, kill an enemy of the State in every ordered society, unless a law forbids it. But there are prohibitions in every State: sacred law, treaties and oaths.

260. Anyone killing any brigand or pirate shall be exempt from penalty, whether he do it by his own hand, or by instigation, or by vote.

261. One must punish wrong-doers to the best of one's ability, and not neglect it. Such conduct is just and good, but the neglect of it is unjust and bad.

262. Those who do what is deserving of exile or imprisonment or other punishment must be condemned and not let off. Whoever contrary to the law acquits a man, judging according to profit or pleasure, does wrong, and this is bound to be on his conscience.

263. He has the greatest share of justice and virtue who awards the greatest offices (*honours?*) (*to the most deserving*).

264. One must not respect the opinion of other men more than one's own; nor must one be more ready to do wrong if no one will know than if all will know. One must respect one's own opinion most, and this must stand as the law of one's soul, preventing one from doing anything improper.

265. Men remember one's mistakes rather than one's successes. This is just; for as those who return a deposit do not deserve praise, whereas those who do not do so deserve blame and punishment, so with the official: he was elected not to make mistakes but to do things well.

266. There is no means under the present constitution by which magistrates can be prevented from wrong-doing, however good they may be. For it is not likely for anyone else

---

[1] For the doubtful words, the MSS. have εὐθυμίης and κτάσεως. Various emendations have been suggested, but none is satisfactory.

(*any more*) than for oneself, that he will show himself the same man in different circumstances.[1]   But we must also make arrangements to see that if a magistrate does no wrong, and convicts wrong-doers, he shall not fall under the power of the latter; rather, a law or some other means must defend the magistrate who does what is just.

267.   Rule belongs by nature to the stronger.

268.   Fear engenders flattery, but it has no good will.

269.   Courage is the beginning of action, but Fortune is the arbiter of the goal.

270.   Use slaves as parts of the body: each to his own function.

271.   A lover's reproach is dissolved by (*? corrupt word*).

272.   The man who is fortunate in his choice of a son-in-law gains a son; the man unfortunate in his choice loses his daughter also.

273.   A woman is far sharper than a man in malign thoughts.

274.   An adornment for a woman is lack of garrulity.   Paucity of adornment is also beautiful.

275.   The rearing of children is full of pitfalls.   Success is attended by strife and care, failure means grief beyond all others.

276.   I do not think that one should have children.   I observe in the acquisition of children many great risks and many griefs, whereas a harvest is rare, and even when it exists, it is thin and poor.

277.   Whoever wants to have children should, in my opinion, choose them from the family of one of his friends.   He will thus obtain a child such as he wishes, for he can select the kind he wants.   And the one that seems fittest will be most likely to follow on his natural endowment.   The difference is that in the latter way one can take one child out of many who is according to one's liking; but if one begets a child of one's own, the risks are many, for one is bound to accept him as he is.

---

[1] *i.e.* power may corrupt even the best.   Diels took τοὺς ἄρχοντας as the object of ἀδικεῖν and translated: 'There is no means of protecting the magistrates from hurt.' He then could make nothing of the next sentence, and was obliged to assume a lacuna.

278. For human beings it is one of the necessities of life to have children, arising from nature and primeval law. It is obvious in the other animals too: they all have offspring by nature, and not for the sake of any profit. And when they are born, the parents work and rear each as best they can and are anxious for them while they are small, and if anything happens to them, the parents are grieved. But for man it has now become an established belief that there should be also some advantage from the offspring.

279. One should, as far as possible, divide out one's property among one's children, at the same time watching over them to see that they do nothing foolish when they have it in their hands. For they thus become much more thrifty over money, and more eager to acquire it and compete with one another. Payments made in a communal establishment do not irk so much as those in a private one, and the income gives much less satisfaction.

280. It is possible without spending much of one's money to educate one's children, and (*so*) to build round their property and their persons a fortification and a safeguard.

281. As among sores canker is the worst disease, so in property . . . (*end lost*).

282. The employment of money with sense is useful towards liberality and justice, but with folly it is a continuous tax that maintains all and sundry (*? reading and meaning uncertain*).

283. Poverty and wealth are terms for lack and superfluity; so that he who lacks is not wealthy, and he who does not lack is not poor.

284. If your desires are not great, a little will seem much to you; for small appetite makes poverty equivalent to wealth.

285. One should realise that human life is weak and brief and mixed with many cares and difficulties, in order that one may care only for moderate possessions, and that hardship may be measured by the standard of one's needs.

286. He is fortunate who is happy with moderate means, unfortunate who is unhappy with great possessions.

287. Communal distress is harder than that of individuals; for there remains no hope of assistance.

288. Disease of the home and of the life comes about in the same way as that of the body.

289. It is unreasonableness not to submit to the necessary conditions of life.

290. Cast forth uncontrollable grief from your benumbed soul by means of reason.

291. To bear poverty well is the sign of a sensible man.

292. The hopes of the unintelligent are senseless.

293. Those to whom their neighbours' misfortunes give pleasure do not understand that the blows of fate are common to all; and also they lack cause for personal joy.

294. The good things of youth are strength and beauty, but the flower of age is moderation.

295. The old man has been young; but the young man cannot know if he will reach old age. Thus the perfected good is better than the uncertain future.

296. Old age is a general mutilation. It possesses everything (*i.e. all the limbs and organs*), but they each lack something.

297. Some men, not knowing about the dissolution of mortal nature, but acting on knowledge of the suffering in life, afflict the period of life with anxieties and fears, inventing false tales about the period after the end of life.

298. (SUIDAS: *Democritus uses the word for 'one's own'*).

Doubtful fragment
298a. Check carefully the passion accumulated in thy breast, and take care not to disturb thy soul, and do not allow all things always to the tongue.[1]

Spurious fragments[2]
298b. (*Title*): '*On the Holy Scripts in Babylon.*'

---

[1] From a Herculanean MS. of Demetrius of Byzantium, who wrote 'On Poetry'. He quotes an unnamed author whom Wilamowitz took to be Democritus, because of the dialect.

[2] For a discussion of these, see *Companion*, pp. 323-5.

299. (*Title*): '*The Babylonian Writings.*' (*Translation of the Pillar of Akikaros.*)

I have travelled most extensively of all men of my time, making the most distant inquiries, and have seen the most climes and lands, and have heard the greatest number of learned men; and no one has ever surpassed me in the composition of treatises with proofs, not even the so-called Arpedonaptae of Egypt; with them I passed eighty[1] years on foreign soil.

(*Titles*)

299a. '*On the Sacred Writings in Meroë.*'

299b. '*Circumnavigation of Ocean.*'

299c. '*On Research.*'

299d. '*Chaldean Theory.*'

299e. '*Phrygian Theory.*'

299f. '*On Fever and those who cough through illness.*'

299g. '*Causes relating to Laws.*'

299h. (*Word meaning* '*Problems*'.)

300. '*The Things Wrought by Hand.*'
'*Potent Natural Products.*'
'*Sympathetic and Antipathetic Substances.*'[2]

301. '*Theogonia.*'

302. *Collection of Maxims.*[3]

302a. (SENECA) One for me is worth the whole populace and the populace worth one.[4]

303. (*Graeco-Syrian Maxims*). Wise men when visiting a foreign land must silently and quietly reconnoitre while they look and listen to find out the reputation of the wise men there: what they are like, and if they can hold their own before them while they secretly weigh their words against their own in their minds. When they have weighed and seen which group is

---

[1] Probably a scribe's mistake for 'five'.
[2] The work of Bolus of Mende, Ch. 78 below.
[3] From the Corpus Parisinum Profanum. Some of these are the same as genuine fragments of Democritus; but many come from other writers, and the collection must be regarded as unauthentic.
[4] Cp. Heracleitus, Frg. 49.

better than the other, then they should make known the riches of their own wisdom, so that they may be prized for the sake of the treasure which is their property, while they enrich others from it. But if their knowledge is too small to allow them to dispense from it, they should take from the others and go their way.[1]

304. (*ib., and Vatican Maxims*) I alone know that I know nothing.

305. (*Reference to Democritus as philosopher in the Arabian writer Qifti*).

306. (*List of 14 titles of books by Democritus in Arabian writer* MASALA, *c.* A.D. 800).

307. (PSEUDORIBASIUS, *a Byzantine forgery: reference to Democritus as writer of aphorisms*).

308. (*Epigram attributed to Democritus; elsewhere to one Metrodorus*).

309. (ALBERTUS MAGNUS: *Democritus said 'Man is the measure of all things that are'*).[2]

69. NESSAS OF CHIOS

NESSAS of CHIOS lived in the fifth and early fourth centuries B.C.

He was said to have been a pupil of Democritus; but the two remaining references to his writings are literary.

1. (*Nessas lengthens a vowel in Homer, disregarding the metre*).

2. (*Nessas derives the word 'Diaktoros' from 'Diagein': 'Conductor of souls'*).

70. MÊTRODÔRUS OF CHIOS

MÊTRODÔRUS of CHIOS lived at some time during the fourth century B.C.

He wrote a book *On Natural Science*; and perhaps works on *The History of Ionia* and *The Trojan War*.

1. None of us knows anything, not even whether we know or do not know, nor do we know whether not knowing and knowing exist, nor in general whether there is anything or not.

---

[1] Gomperz regarded this as genuine.   [2] Protagoras, Frg. 1.

2. Everything exists which anyone perceives.

3-5. *(From a work on 'The Trojan War').*

3. *(Marsyas discovered the reed-pipe among the Celaenae).*

4. *(Divine visitants command that an acropolis shall be built for the Spartan king, in which he is to live).*

5. *(Grammatical comment on Homer, ascribed to 'Metrodorus', who may be Metrodorus of Lampsacus).*

6. *(History of Ionia: the people of Smyrna, who are Aeolians by origin, sacrifice a black bull to Boubrôstis: they cut it up and burn it, hide and all).*

71. DIOGENES OF SMYRNA

Diogenes of Smyrna lived in the fourth century B.C.

His opinions, which are said to have been the same as those of Protagoras, have not survived.

72. ANAXARCHUS OF ABDÊRA

Anaxarchus of Abdêra was in his prime about 340 B.C., and was active throughout the reign of Alexander.

He wrote a book *On Monarchy*.

1. Much learning can help much, but also can greatly harm him who has it. It helps the clever man, but harms him who readily utters every word in any company. One must know the measure of the right time, for this is the boundary of wisdom. Those who recite a saying outside the right time, even if their saying is wise, are reproached with folly, because they do not mix intelligence with wisdom.

2. *(From the work 'On Monarchy')*: It is hard to collect money, but harder still to keep it safely.

73. HECATAEUS OF ABDÊRA

Hecataeus of Abdêra lived at the end of the fourth and the beginning of the third centuries B.C.

He was credited with books *On the Hyperboreans* and *On the Philosophy of the Egyptians*. A work *On the Jews* was also attributed to him.

(From 'On the Hyperboreans').

1. *(Elixoia, island of the Hyperboreans, lies beyond the river Karambyka; the islanders are named Karambykae from the river).*

2. *(Hecataeus calls the Northern Ocean 'Amalchius' from the River Parapanisus onward, which river irrigates Scythia: the name 'Amalchius' in Scythian means 'frozen').*

3. *(He celebrated the Hyperboreans and their worship of Apollo).*

4. *(Hecataeus says that the Hyperboreans survived to his day. They worship Apollo, who has been seen visiting them. There are three branches of Hyperboreans).*

5. *(Hecataeus and others say that in the place opposite the Celtic land, in the ocean, is an island not smaller than Sicily; this belongs to the north, and is inhabited by the so-called Hyperboreans. It is fertile and productive and of fine climate, and has two crops a year.*
    They say that the moon, being only a short distance away, can be completely seen, and has several earthy projections clearly visible. It is said that Apollo visits the island every 19th year, and this is called by the Greeks a Great Year, when all the constellations are completing their journeys. On his appearance, the god plays the harp and dances all night long, from the spring equinox to the rise of the Pleiades, enjoying his own fine weather. This State is ruled by the Boreadae, who are descendants of Boreas; and the offices are hereditary).

(From the work 'On the Philosophy of the Egyptians').

6. *(The Egyptians speak riddlingly of their gods in the form of beetle, serpent, hawk etc., as Manetho and Hecataeus say. Hecataeus says that the Magi say that the gods 'come into being'. The Magi preach immortality for men).*

7. *(Diodorus' account of Egyptian theology, thought to be partly drawn from Hecataeus).*

8. *(Hecataeus says that 'Ammon' is not a particular name given to Zeus, but a way of calling the premier god and summoning him to appear).*

9. *(Heracleitus and Hecataeus say that the sun is a wet flame from the sea).*

10. *(Tnephachthos while on a campaign, being obliged to eat with*

ordinary men, enjoyed the fare so much that ever afterwards he was hostile to luxury and cursed the King who had introduced it. The curse was written up on the Temple of Zeus at Thebes in hieroglyphics).

11. (The ministrants at Heliopolis do not take wine into the temple. Others use it, but sparingly. There are many wineless rites. The Pharaohs, being priests, used to drink an amount specified in the holy writings).

12. (Diodorus states that Hecataeus is one of those Greeks who have written a History of Egypt, and who agree with his account of the Theban dynasty).

13. (Photius says that Diodorus' account of the history, laws and customs of the Jews are false, but that he hides behind Hecataeus).

13a. (The greatness of Egyptian Thebes before its destruction by Persia: figures of Hecataeus are quoted. The Thebaid contained 13,030 villages, 7 million men, etc. There were four other small 'cities of Zeus', in one of which they kept crocodiles in caves and wells, and never tasted the water of the river whatever their need).

(From a grammatical work, which Diodorus also quotes)

14. (Kyrbasiê, the so-called tiara: Hecataeus says that the comic poets call it a 'barbarian cap').

Forged writings
15. (Titles given by Josephus: 'On the Jews' or 'On Abraham').

16. (ORIGEN: A book on the Jews under the name of Hecataeus is in circulation, in which he insists so much on the wisdom of the race that Philo doubts if the treatise is by Hecataeus, or, if it is his, says that he must have been captivated by Jewish persuasiveness and have accepted their arguments).

17. (The references in Agatharchus the historian to Hecataeus of Abdera belong to Hecataeus of Miletus).[1]

74. APOLLODŌRUS OF CYZICUS

APOLLODŌRUS of CYZICUS: date unknown.
Follower of Democritus. No writings preserved.

[1] Müller, F.H.G. I., 14, 1, 13.

75. NAUSIPHANES OF TEOS

Nausiphanes of Teos lived in the time of Alexander, and after.

He wrote a book called *The Tripod*, on epistemology and method. This was said to have been the source of Epicurus' *Canon*. It is preserved in epitome only, by Philodemus.

1. (*The man of science has the capacity for rhetoric, even if he does not practise it*).

2. (*The wise man will pursue rhetoric, because honour depends on winning a reputation for cleverness in politics, rather than on the over-lauded virtues.*

The wise man is he who can persuade his hearers; this power belongs to the man of science, its source being his knowledge of the facts, so that he could pass on his own convictions not only to his pupils but to any race of people. Having a knowledge of the facts, he is able to lead his audience where he wishes, because he can tell them what is to their advantage, which is what they wish to hear. The scientist has command of the best diction also: not that created by vain imagination and usage, but that based on the nature of things. He also has command of logic, without which knowledge is impossible, and is best qualified in that art indispensable to a statesman in a democracy or monarchy or any other constitution, of calculation of the future from the known facts.

The man who employs continuous discourse will be best able to employ the dialectic method and vice versa, because both depend on an accurate judgement of how to lead pupils from the known to the unknown; that is, they depend upon a knowledge of the 'right time' and 'right measure' in speaking).

3. (*Nausiphanes gave 'immovability' as the goal of life, this being the name he gave to Democritus' 'imperturbability'*).

4. (*Of those things which appear to exist, nothing exists more than it does not exist*).

76. DIOTÎMUS OF TYRE

Diotîmus of Tyre: exact date unknown.

A follower of Democritus. No writings survive.

77. BIÔN OF ABDÊRA

Biôn of Abdêra probably lived at the end of the fourth century B.C.

A follower of Democritus. He wrote on meteorology, but none of his writings survive.

78. BÔLUS OF MENDÊ

Bôlus of Mendê in the Nile Delta, lived in the third century B.C.

He wrote works on *Potent Natural Products*, and on *Antipathetic and Sympathetic Substances*, which were often ascribed to Democritus; these were books of magic remedies. He also wrote other works of magical doctrine, on alchemy and divination.

79. THE OLDER SOPHISTS: NAME AND CONCEPT

The Older Sophists: Name and Concept. These men were active during the latter part of the fifth and early part of the fourth centuries B.C.

'Sophistês' originally meant 'skilled craftsman' or 'wise man'. The specialised meaning 'professional teacher' did not come into use until the end of the fifth century B.C., the period of the travelling teachers. The bad sense of the word developed almost immediately; Aristotle summed up the Sophist's art as 'the appearance, not the reality, of wisdom', and the Sophist as one who makes money out of this pretence.

The title was nevertheless used in Roman Imperial times for 'professor' of rhetoric, or prose writer, without any bad meaning.

80. PRÔTAGORAS OF ABDÊRA

Prôtagoras of Abdêra: latter half of fifth century B.C.

He wrote a book called *Truth* or *Refutatory Arguments* or *On Being*; and one *On the Gods*. Various other titles are mentioned.

1. (*From 'Truth' or 'Refutatory Arguments'*). Of all things the measure is Man, of the things that are, that they are, and of the things that are not, that they are not.

2. (*From 'On Being'*).

(Porphyry: '*Few of the writings of Plato's predecessors have survived, otherwise Plato perhaps would have been detected in further plagiarisms. At any rate, in the place where I happened to have been reading in Protagoras' book "On Being" the argument he uses against those who make Being One, I find that he uses the same refutatory terms. For I took the trouble to memorise the passage word for word*').

3. (*From a treatise entitled 'Great Logos'*). Teaching needs endowment and practice. Learning must begin in youth.

4. (*From 'On the Gods'*). About the gods, I am not able to know whether they exist or do not exist, nor what they are like in form; for the factors preventing knowledge are many: the obscurity of the subject, and the shortness of human life.

5. (*Title: 'Contradictory Arguments'. Plato plagiarised from this in the 'Republic'*).

Doubtful titles (taken from Diogenes Laertius)
6. (*'Art of the Eristics': disputations on famous subjects. Protagoras and the other Sophists were the first to compose these set pieces known as 'common-places'*).

6a. (*Protagoras was the first to say that there were two contradictory arguments about everything*).

6b. To make the weaker cause the stronger.

'On Mathematics'
7. (*Protagoras, arguing against the definition of the mathematicians and appealing to perception, used to say that the tangent touched the circle not at a point but along a line*).

'On Wrestling and the Other Arts'
8. (PLATO, *Sophist* 232D, E: *'Those views regarding all the arts and each art separately, what one must say against the craftsman practising each: views which stand published in writing for all to learn if they wish. — I think you must mean the views of Protagoras on wrestling and the other arts'*).

(Titles)
8a. *'On Constitution.'*

8b. *'On the Original Social Structure.'*

8c. *'On Ambition.'*

8d. *'On Virtues.'*

8e. *'On Human Errors.'*

8f. *'Exhortation.'*

8g. *'Trial concerning a Fee.'*

8h. *'On the Underworld.'*

From unspecified writings

9.   When his sons, who were fine young men, died within eight days, he (Pericles) bore it without mourning. For he held on to his serenity, from which every day he derived great benefit in happiness, freedom from suffering, and honour in the people's eyes — for all who saw him bearing his griefs valiantly thought him great-souled and brave and superior to themselves, well knowing their own helplessness in such a calamity.

10.   Art without practice, and practice without art, are nothing.

11.   Education does not take root in the soul unless one goes deep.

12.   (*Graeco-Syrian Maxims: Protagoras said*): Toil and work and instruction and education and wisdom are the garland of fame which is woven from the flowers of an eloquent tongue and set on the head of those who love it. Eloquence however is difficult, yet its flowers are rich and ever new, and the audience and those who applaud and the teachers rejoice, and the scholars make progress and fools are vexed — or perhaps they are not even vexed, because they have not sufficient insight.

81. XENIADES OF CORINTH

XENIADES of CORINTH: date unknown.
   He took up a position of extreme nihilism in knowledge. No writings survive.

82. GORGIAS OF LEONTÎNI

GORGIAS of LEONTÎNI: latter half of fifth century B.C.
   He wrote one of the earliest Handbooks on Rhetoric; an essay *On Being* or *On Nature*; and a number of model orations, of which parts have survived: from the Olympian Oration, the *Encomium on Helen*, and the *Defence of Palamêdês*.

1.   (ISOCRATES: *Gorgias had the hardihood to say that nothing whatever exists*).

2. (OLYMPIODORUS: *Gorgias wrote a treatise 'On Nature', not without skill, in the 84th Olympiad*).[1]

3. (SEXTUS, *from 'On Being' or 'On Nature'*):

I.   Nothing exists.

    (*a*) Not-Being does not exist.

    (*b*) Being does not exist.

        i. as everlasting.

        ii. as created.

        iii. as both.

        iv. as One.

        v. as Many.

    (*c*) A mixture of Being and Not-Being does not exist.

II.   If anything exists, it is incomprehensible.

III.   If it is comprehensible, it is incommunicable.

I.   Nothing exists.

If anything exists, it must be either Being or Not-Being, or both Being and Not-Being.

(*a*) It cannot be Not-Being, for Not-Being does not exist; if it did, it would be at the same time Being and Not-Being, which is impossible.

(*b*) It cannot be Being, for Being does not exist. If Being exists, it must be either everlasting, or created, or both.

i. It cannot be everlasting; if it were, it would have no beginning, and therefore would be boundless; if it is boundless, then it has no position, for if it had position it would be contained in something, and so it would no longer be boundless; for that which contains is greater than that which is contained; and nothing is greater than the boundless. It cannot be contained by itself, for then the thing containing and the thing contained would be the same, and Being would become two things — both position and body — which is absurd. Hence if Being is everlasting, it is boundless; if boundless, it has no position ('is nowhere'); if without position, it does not exist.

ii. Similarly, Being cannot be created; if it were, it must come from something, either Being or Not-Being, both of which are impossible.

iii. Similarly, Being cannot be both everlasting and created, since they are opposite. Therefore Being does not exist.

iv. Being cannot be One, because if it exists it has size, and is therefore infinitely divisible; at least it is threefold, having length, breadth and depth.

v. It cannot be Many, because the Many is made up of an addition of Ones, so that since the One does not exist, the Many do not exist either.

(*c*) A mixture of Being and Not-Being is impossible. Therefore since Being does not exist, nothing exists.

II. If anything exists, it is incomprehensible.

If the concepts of the mind are not realities, reality cannot be thought: if the thing thought is white, then white is thought about; if the thing thought is non-existent, then non-existence is thought about; this is equivalent to saying that 'existence, reality, is not thought about, cannot be thought'. Many things thought about are not realities: we can conceive of a chariot running on the sea, or a winged man. Also, since things seen are the objects of sight, and things heard are the objects of hearing, and we accept as real things seen without their being heard, and vice versa; so we would have to accept things thought without their being seen or heard; but this would mean believing in things like the chariot racing on the sea.

Therefore reality is not the object of thought, and cannot be comprehended by it. Pure mind, as opposed to sense-perception, or even as an equally valid criterion, is a myth.

III. If anything is comprehensible, it is incommunicable.

The things which exist are perceptibles; the objects of sight are apprehended by sight, the objects of hearing by hearing, and there is no interchange; so that these sense-perceptions cannot communicate with one another. Further, that with which we communicate is speech, and speech is not the same thing as the things that exist, the perceptibles; so that we communicate not the things which exist, but only speech; just as that which is seen cannot become that which is heard, so our speech cannot be equated with that which exists, since it is outside us. Further, speech is composed from the percepts which we receive from without, that is, from perceptibles; so that it is not speech which communicates perceptibles, but perceptibles which create speech. Further, speech can never exactly represent perceptibles, since it is different from them, and perceptibles are apprehended each by the one kind of organ, speech by another. Hence, since the objects of sight cannot be presented to any other organ but sight, and the different sense-organs cannot give their information to one another, similarly speech cannot give any information about perceptibles.

Therefore, if anything exists and is comprehended, it is incommunicable.

4. (PLATO *in the 'Meno'*, 76A *sqq.: colour is an effluence from objects, fitting the passages of the eyes*).

5. (*Explanation of the power of the burning-glass*): The fire goes out through the pores.

5a. (*From the 'Funeral Oration'*. *Extravagant expressions*): Xerxes, the Persian Zeus.
Vultures, living tombs.

5b. (*From the 'Funeral Oration'*). Trophies (*victories*) against barbarians demand hymns of praise, but those against Greeks, lamentations.

6. (*From the 'Funeral Oration': typical passage of antitheses*): For what did these men lack that men should have? What did they have that men should not have? Would that I could express what I wish, and may I wish what I ought, avoiding divine wrath, shunning human envy! For the courage these men possessed was divine, and the mortal part (*alone*) was human. Often, indeed, they preferred mild reasonableness to harsh justice, often also correctness of speech to exactitude of law, holding that the most divine and most generally applicable law was to say or keep silent, do or not do, the necessary thing at the necessary moment. They doubly exercised, above all, as was right, mind and body, the one in counsel, the other in action; helpers of those in undeserved adversity, chastisers of those in undeserved prosperity; bold for the common good, quick to feel for the right cause, checking with the prudence of the mind the imprudence of the body; violent towards the violent, restrained towards the restrained, fearless towards the fearless, terrifying among the terrifying. As evidence of these things, they have set up trophies over the enemy, an honour to Zeus, a dedication of themselves: men not unacquainted with the inborn spirit of the warrior, with love such as the law allows, with rivalry under arms, with peace, friend of the arts; men showing reverence towards the gods by their justice, piety towards their parents by their care, justice towards their fellow-citizens by their fair dealing, respect towards their friends by keeping faith with them. Therefore, although they are dead, the longing for them has not died with them, but immortal though in mortal bodies, it lives on for those who live no more.

(*From the 'Olympian Oration'*)
7. (*The Conveners of the Festival*) deserve admiration from many, men of Hellas!

8. Our struggle demands two virtues, courage and wisdom: to courage belongs endurance of danger, and to wisdom, the knowledge of (*the right way to tackle it*).[1]

---

[1] πλίγμα 'hold in wrestling', emendation of Diels from MSS. αἴνιγμα, 'riddle'.

8a. (*Gorgias advised the Greeks on Concord in his 'Olympian Oration,' but could not bring about concord between himself, his wife and his maid*).

9. (*'Pythian Oration': no remains*).

10. (*Opening sentence of the 'Encomium on the Eleans'*): Elis is a fortunate city.

11. (*'Encomium on Helen': summary*)

(1) The glory (*cosmos*) of a city is courage, of a body, beauty, of a soul, wisdom, of action, virtue, of speech, truth; it is right in all circumstances to praise what is praiseworthy and blame what is blameworthy.

(2) It belongs to the same man both to speak the truth and to refute falsehood. Helen is universally condemned and regarded as the symbol of disasters; I wish to subject her story to critical examination, and so rescue her from ignorant calumny.

(3) She was of the highest parentage: her reputed father Tyndareus was the most powerful of men; her real father, Zeus, was king of all.

(4) From these origins she obtained her divine beauty, by the display of which she inspired love in countless men, and caused the assemblage of a great number of ambitious suitors, some endowed with wealth, others with ancestral fame, others with personal prowess, others with accumulated wisdom.

(5) I shall not relate the story of who won Helen or how: to tell an audience what it knows wins belief but gives no pleasure. I shall pass over this period and come to the beginning of my defence, setting out the probable reasons for her journey to Troy.

(6) She acted as she did either through Fate and the will of the gods and the decrees of Necessity, or because she was seized by force, or won over by persuasion (*or captivated by love*). If the first, it is her accuser who deserves blame; for no human foresight can hinder the will of God: the stronger cannot be hindered by the weaker, and God is stronger than man in every way. Therefore if the cause was Fate, Helen cannot be blamed.

(7) If she was carried off by force, clearly her abductor wronged her and she was unfortunate. He, a barbarian, com-

mitted an act of barbarism, and should receive blame, disgrace and punishment; she, being robbed of her country and friends, deserves pity rather than obloquy.

(8) If it was speech that persuaded her and deceived her soul, her defence remains easy. Speech is a great power, which achieves the most divine works by means of the smallest and least visible form; for it can even put a stop to fear, remove grief, create joy, and increase pity. This I shall now prove:

(9) All poetry can be called speech in metre. Its hearers shudder with terror, shed tears of pity, and yearn with sad longing; the soul, affected by the words, feels as its own an emotion aroused by the good and ill fortunes of other people's actions and lives.

(10) The inspired incantations of words can induce pleasure and avert grief; for the power of the incantations, uniting with the feeling in the soul, soothes and persuades and transports by means of its wizardry. Two types of wizardry and magic have been invented, which are errors in the soul and deceptions in the mind.

(11) Their persuasions by means of fictions are innumerable; for if everyone had recollection of the past, knowledge of the present, and foreknowledge of the future, the power of speech would not be so great. But as it is, when men can neither remember the past nor observe the present nor prophesy the future, deception is easy; so that most men offer opinion as advice to the soul. But opinion, being unreliable, involves those who accept it in equally uncertain fortunes.

(12) (*Text corrupt*) Thus, persuasion by speech is equivalent to abduction by force, as she was compelled to agree to what was said, and consent to what was done. It was therefore the persuader, not Helen, who did wrong and should be blamed.

(13) That Persuasion, when added to speech, can also make any impression it wishes on the soul, can be shown, firstly, from the arguments of the meteorologists, who by removing one opinion and implanting another, cause what is incredible and invisible to appear before the eyes of the mind; secondly, from legal contests, in which a speech can sway and persuade a crowd, by the skill of its composition, not by the truth of its statements; thirdly, from the philosophical debates, in which quickness of thought is shown easily altering opinion.

(14) The power of speech over the constitution of the soul can be compared with the effect of drugs on the bodily state: just as drugs by driving out different humours from the body can put an end either to the disease or to life, so with speech: different words can induce grief, pleasure or fear; or again, by means of a harmful kind of persuasion, words can drug and bewitch the soul.

(15) If Helen was persuaded by love, defence is equally easy. What we see has its own nature, not chosen by us; and the soul is impressed through sight.

(16) For instance, in war, the sight of enemy forms wearing hostile array is so disturbing to the soul that often men flee in terror as if the coming danger were already present. The powerful habit induced by custom is displaced by the fear aroused by sight, which causes oblivion of what custom judges honourable and of the advantage derived from victory.

(17) People who have seen a frightful sight have been driven out of their minds, so great is the power of fear; while many have fallen victims to useless toils, dreadful diseases and incurable insanity, so vivid are the images of the things seen which vision engraves on the mind.

(18) Painters, however, when they create one shape from many colours, give pleasure to sight; and the pleasure afforded by sculpture to the eyes is divine; many objects engender in many people a love of many actions and forms.

(19) If therefore Helen's eye, delighted with Paris's form, engendered the passion of love in her soul, this is not remarkable; for if a god is at work with divine power, how can the weaker person resist him? And if the disease is human, due to the soul's ignorance, it must not be condemned as a crime but pitied as a misfortune, for it came about through the snares of Fate, not the choice of the will; by the compulsion of love, not by the plottings of art.

(20) Therefore, whichever of the four reasons caused Helen's action, she is innocent.

(21) I have expunged by my discourse this woman's ill fame, and have fulfilled the object set forth at the outset. I have tried to destroy the unjust blame and the ignorant opinion, and have chosen to write this speech as an Encomium on Helen and an amusement for myself.

11a. *(The 'Defence of Palamêdês': summary).*[1]

(1)   This trial is concerned not with death, which comes to all, but with honour: whether I am to die justly or unjustly, under a load of disgrace.

(2)   You have the power to decide the issue; you can kill me easily if you wish, whereas I am powerless.

(3)   If the accuser Odysseus were bringing the charge because he knew or believed me to be betraying Greece to the barbarians, he would be the best of men, as ensuring the safety of his country, his parents and all Greece, as well as the punishment of the traitor; but if he has concocted this charge through malice, he is equally the worst of men.

(4)   Where shall I begin my defence? A cause unsupported by proof engenders fear, and fear makes speech difficult, unless truth and necessity instruct me — teachers more productive of risk than of the means of help.

(5)   The accuser cannot know for certain that I committed the crime, because I know for certain that I did not. But if he is acting on conjecture, I can prove in two ways that he is wrong.

(6)   First, I cannot have committed the crime. Treasonable action must begin with discussion; but discussion implies a meeting, which was impossible since no one could come to me and I could not go to anyone, nor could a written message be sent.

(7)   Nor was direct communication possible between myself, a Greek, and the enemy, a barbarian, since we did not understand each other's language, and an interpreter would have meant having an accomplice.

(8)   But even supposing communication could have been arranged, it would have been necessary to exchange pledges, such as hostages (which was impossible),

(9)   or perhaps money. A small sum would not have sufficed in such a great undertaking; a large sum could not have been transported without the help of many confederates.

(10)   Conveyance of money would have been impossible at night because of the guards, and by daylight because all could see. Nor could I have gone out, or the enemy have come into the camp. Nor could I have concealed any money received.

---

[1] This speech has at first sight little philosophical interest; but its influence on forensic oratory, and therefore doubtless on education, cannot be over-estimated.

(11) But suppose all this achieved — communication established and pledges exchanged — action had then to follow. This had to be done with or without confederates. If with confederates, were they free or slaves? If any free man has information, let him speak. Slaves are always untrustworthy: they accuse voluntarily to win freedom, and also under compulsion when tortured.

(12) Nor could the enemy have entered by my help, either by the gates or over the walls, because of the guards; nor could I have breached the walls, as in camp everybody sees everything. Therefore all such action was completely impossible for me.

(13) What motive could I have had? Absolute power over yourselves or the barbarians? The former is impossible in view of your courage, wealth, prowess of body and mind, control of cities.

(14) Rulership over the barbarian is equally impossible. I could not have seized it or won it by persuasion, nor would they have handed it to me voluntarily: no one would choose slavery instead of kingship, the worst instead of the best.

(15) Nor was wealth my motive. I have moderate means, and do not need more. Wealth is needed by those who spend much; not by those who are masters of their natural pleasures, but by those who are enslaved by pleasures, or wish to buy honour with riches. I call you to witness that my past life proves me not to be one of these.

(16) My motive cannot have been ambition: honour accrues to virtue, not to a betrayer of Greece. Besides, I had honour already, from you for my wisdom.

(17) Safety cannot have been the motive. The traitor is the enemy of all: law, justice, the gods, his fellow-men.

(18) Another motive could be the desire to help friends and injure enemies; but I would have been doing the reverse.

(19) The remaining possibility would be a wish to avoid trouble or danger. But if I betrayed Greece, I should have betrayed myself and all that I had.

(20) My life would have been unbearable in Greece; and if I stayed among the barbarians, I would have thrown away all the rewards of my past labours, through my own action, which is worst.

(21) The barbarians too would have distrusted me; and if

one loses credit, life is intolerable. The loss of money or throne or country can be retrieved; but the loss of credit is irretrievable. It is thus proved that I neither could nor would have betrayed Greece.

(22) I now address my accuser: do you base your accusation on knowledge or conjecture? If on knowledge, either this is your own or hearsay. If it is your own, give exact details of time, place, method; if hearsay, produce your witness.

(23) It is your place to produce witnesses, not mine: no witness can be produced for what did not happen; but for what did happen, it is easy and essential to produce witnesses. But you cannot produce even false witnesses.

(24) That you have no knowledge of your accusations is clear. Hence they must be conjectural, and you are the most villainous of men, to bring a capital charge relying on opinion — which is a most unreliable thing — and not knowing the truth. Conjecture is open to all in everything, and you are no wiser than anyone else in this. One must believe, not conjecture, but truth.

(25) You are accusing me of two opposites, wisdom and madness: wisdom in that I am crafty, clever, resourceful; madness in that I wished to betray Greece. It is madness to attempt what is impossible, disadvantageous, disgraceful, injurious to friends and helpful to enemies, and likely to make one's life intolerable. But how can one believe a man who in the same speech, to the same audience, says the exact opposite about the same things?

(26) Do you consider the wise to be foolish or sensible? If you say 'foolish', this is original but untrue. If 'sensible', then sensible men do not commit the greatest crimes, or prefer evil to the good they have. If I am wise, I did not err. If I erred, I am not wise. Therefore you are proved a liar on both counts.

(27) I could bring counter-accusations, but I will not. I would rather seek acquittal through my virtues than your vices.

(28) (*To the jury*): I must now speak of myself, in a way that would not be suitable except to one accused. I submit my past life to your scrutiny. If I mention my good deeds, I pray that no one will resent this: it is necessary in order that I may refute serious charges with a true statement of merits known to you.

(29)   Above all, my past life has been blameless. My accuser can bring no proof of this charge, so that his speech is unsubstantiated obloquy.

(30)   I claim also to be a benefactor of Greece, present and future, by reason of my inventions, in tactics, law, letters (the tool of memory), measures (arbiters of business dealings), number (the guardian of property), beacon-fires (the best and swiftest messengers), and the game of draughts as a pastime.

(31)   I mention these things to show that in devoting my thoughts to them I am bound to abstain from wicked deeds.

(32)   I deserve no punishment from young or old. I have been considerate to the old, helpful to the young, without envy of the prosperous, merciful to the distressed; not despising poverty, nor preferring wealth to virtue; useful in counsel, active in war, fulfilling commands, obeying the rulers. But it is not for me to praise myself; I do so under the compulsion of self-defence.

(33)   Lastly I shall speak of you to you. Lamentations, prayers, and the petitions of friends are useful when judgement depends on the mob; but before you, the foremost of the Greeks, I need not use these devices, but only justice and truth.

(34)   You must not heed words rather than facts, nor prefer accusations to proof, nor regard a brief period as more instructive than a long one, nor consider calumny more trustworthy than experience. Good men avoid all wrong-doing, but above all what cannot be mended; things can be righted by forethought, but are irrevocable by afterthought. This happens when men are trying a fellow-man on a capital charge, as you now are.

(35)   If words could bring the truth of deeds clearly and certainly before their hearers, judgement would be easy; since this is not so, I ask you to preserve my life, await the passage of time, and pass your judgement with truth. You run the great risk of a reputation for injustice; to good men, death is preferable to a bad reputation: one is the end of life, the other is a disease in life.

(36)   If you put me to death unjustly, you will bear the blame in the eyes of all Greece, as I am not unknown and you are famous. The blame will be yours, not my accuser's, because the issue is in your hands. There could be no greater

crime than if you as Greeks put to death a Greek, an ally, a benefactor of yours and of Greece, when you can show no cause.

(37)   Here I stop. A summary of a long speech is worth while when one is speaking to a jury of inferiors; but before the leaders of Greece it is uncalled-for, as is the exhortation to pay attention or to remember what has been said.

12.   One must destroy one's adversaries' seriousness with laughter, and their laughter with seriousness.

13.   (*No one, not even Gorgias who first wrote on the subject, has defined the art of 'the right moment'*).

14.   (*Gorgias gave his pupils model speeches to learn by heart*).

From unspecified writings
15.   Beggarly toadying bards, who swear a false oath and swear it well.

16.   Affairs are pale, tremulous and anaemic; you have sown in this a shameful seed, and will reap an evil harvest.

17.   (*My*) matter never fails (*in speaking*).

18.   (*Gorgias enumerated the virtues instead of defining them*).

19.   (PLATO, *Meno* 71E: *examples of enumeration of virtues, after the teaching of Gorgias*).

20.   Cimon acquired money in order to use it, and used it to acquire honour.

21.   A friend will expect his friend to do only just actions in helping him; but he himself will serve his friend with many actions that belong to the category of unjust also.

22.   Not the looks of a woman, but her good reputation should be known to many.

23.   Tragedy, by means of legends and emotions, creates a deception in which the deceiver is more honest than the non-deceiver, and the deceived is wiser than the non-deceived.

24.   (*The 'Seven against Thebes' of Aeschylus*): Full of Ares.

25.   (*Homer's descent traced to Musaeus*).

26. Being is unrecognisable unless it succeeds in seeming, and seeming is weak unless it succeeds in being.

27. Threats were mixed with supplications, and lamentations with prayers.

Doubtful

28. (*Graeco-Syrian Maxims: Gor(gon)ias said*): The surpassing beauty of something hidden is shown when skilled painters cannot depict it with their tried colours. Their work and their effort affords a wonderful proof of the hidden magnificence. And when the separate stages of their work come to an end, they give to it the crown of victory in that they are silent. But that which no hand grasps and no eye sees, how can the tongue express it or the ear of the hearer receive it?

29. Those who neglect philosophy and spend their time on ordinary studies are like the Suitors who desired Penelope but slept with her maids.

30. Orators are like frogs: the latter sing in the water, the former to the water-clock.

31. The sun is a molten mass.

83. LYCOPHRŌN 'THE SOPHIST'

LYCOPHRŌN 'THE SOPHIST': birthplace unknown; lived probably in the first half of the fourth century B.C.

An orator of the school of Gorgias; interested also in metaphysics, political science and politics.

1.) Knowledge is an association between the act of knowing and the soul.

2. (*He eliminated the verb 'is' in predication*).

3. Law is a guarantor of mutual justice.

4. The beauty of high birth is hidden, its dignity merely a matter of words.

5. The varying-featured heaven of the mighty-peaked earth. The narrow-channelled shore. Xerxes, monstrous man. Sciron the ravager.

84. PRODICUS OF CEOS

PRODICUS of CEOS lived in the latter half of the fifth century B.C.

He wrote on correct terminology, and was credited with a book *On Nature*, or *On the Nature of Man*. He also wrote exercises on set themes, meant for display, one of which, *The Choice of Heracles*, was paraphrased by Xenophon in the *Memorabilia*, and mentioned by Plato in the *Symposium*.

1. (SCHOLIAST on Aristophanes, *Clouds: The book describing the Choice of Heracles is called 'Horae'*).

2. (XENOPHON, *Memorabilia*, II.1.21: *The Choice of Heracles. Heracles, having come to the time when the young choose their way of life, is confronted by two women, Virtue and Vice, who set before him the rival claims of the way of pleasure and the way of honourable toil*).

3. (*Title: 'On the Nature of Things'*).

4. (GALEN: *Prodicus in his book 'On the Nature of Man' called the heated and as it were overcooked element in the bodily humours the 'phlegm', and the mucous discharge which is universally named 'phlegm' he called 'blenna', 'slime'*).

5. (*Things from which benefits to human life have been derived have come to be considered deities, such as Demeter and Dionysus*).

6. (*Sophists are*) on the borderline between the philosopher and the statesman.

7. Desire when doubled is love, love when doubled is madness.

Doubtful

8. (Ps.-PLATO, *Eryxias* 397D: *Prodicus said that things were good or bad according to their users, for example, wealth*).

9. (Ps.-PLATO, *Axiochus* 366B: *Prodicus teaches nothing free*).

Spurious

10. Fire is the best of the perfumes.

11. Milk is best if one draw it actually from the female.

85. THRASYMACHUS OF CHALCÊDÔN

THRASYMACHUS of CHALCÊDÔN was active in the latter half of the fifth century B.C.

He left a large number of writings: a *Great Text-book*; *Subjects for Oratory*; *Prooemia*; *Preponderances*; and other works connected with Rhetoric. One long example of his style is preserved from one of his 'public orations', written as an exercise.

1. I could wish, men of Athens, to have belonged to that long-past time when the young were content to remain silent unless events compelled them to speak, and while the older men were correctly supervising affairs of State. But since Fate has so far advanced us in time that we must obey others as rulers but must suffer the consequences ourselves; and when the worst results are not the work of Heaven or Fate but of our administrators, then it is necessary to speak. A man either has no feeling, or has too much patience, if he is willing to go on offering himself up to whoever wishes as the object of their mistakes, and is ready to take on himself the blame for the guile and wickedness of others.

No, the past is enough for us — that we have exchanged peace for war, reaching the present through dangers, so that we regard the past with affection and the future with fear; and that we have sacrificed concord for enmity and internal disturbance. Others are driven to excesses and civil strife through a surfeit of prosperity; but we behaved soberly in our prosperity. We were seized with madness at a time of adversity, which usually makes others act soberly. Why then should anyone delay to say what he knows, if he happens to feel grief at the present state of affairs, and to believe that he has a means of bringing this to an end?

First of all, therefore, I shall prove in my speech that those of the orators and others who are at variance are mutually experiencing something that is bound to befall those who engage in senseless rivalry: believing that they are expressing opposite views, they fail to perceive that their actions are the same, and that the theory of the opposite party is inherent in their own theory. For consider from the beginning what each party is seeking.

In the first place, the 'ancestral constitution' is a cause of dissension between them, though it is easiest to grasp and is the common property of all citizens. Whatever lies outside our knowledge must necessarily be learnt from earlier generations, but whatever the elder generation has itself witnessed, we can find out from those who know.

2. (*From a speech 'On behalf of the people of Larissa'*): Shall we who are Greeks be the slaves of Archelaus a barbarian?

3. (*Title: 'The Great Text-book'*).

4. (*From the 'Prooemia': Timocreon,*[1] *entertained by the Great King, ate so much that the King inquired his purpose; Timocreon replied, 'To thrash innumerable Persians'. Next day, having beaten numbers of them one after another, he went on to shadow-boxing; asked why, he said that these were the blows left over for any fresh competitor*).

5. (*Thrasymachus in his 'Appeals to Compassion' wrote on the art of delivery*).

6. (PLATO, *Phaedrus* 267C: *Thrasymachus claimed to be able to arouse anger in many, and then allay their anger with charms and incantations*).

6a. (PLATO, *Republic* 338C: *Thrasymachus speaking*): Justice is nothing other than the advantage of the stronger.

7. (*Title: 'Preponderant Arguments'*).

7a. (*Thrasymachus and others mistakenly believed that they possessed the art of political and public oratory*).

From unspecified writing
8. The gods do not see human affairs; otherwise they would not have overlooked the greatest of all blessings among mankind, Justice — for we see mankind not using this virtue.

86. HIPPIAS OF ÊLIS

HIPPIAS of ÊLIS was active in the second half of the fifth century B.C.
Various writings are attributed to him, of which almost nothing survives. He was probably the discoverer of the curve called *quadratrix*, the construction of which is preserved in Proclus' *Commentary on Euclid*.[2]

[1] Lyric poet of Rhodes, sixth-fifth centuries B.C., famous for large appetite, great strength, and invective.
[2] See *Companion*, pp. 385-8.

1. (PAUSANIAS: *Hippias wrote the elegiac inscription on the bronze statues of those who were drowned when the boys' choir was lost on the crossing between Messene and Rhegium*).

2. (*From a work entitled 'Nomenclature of Tribes': mention of a tribe called Spartoi*).

3. (*List of victors at Olympia*).

4. (*From a work entitled 'Collection': Thargêlia of Miletus distinguished for beauty and wisdom, was married fourteen times*).

5. (*Title: 'Trojan Dialogue'*).

From unspecified writings

6. Some of these things may have been said by Orpheus some by Musaeus, briefly in different places, some by Hesiod and Homer, others by others of the poets, some in the prose writings of the Greeks. I have put together the most important and homogeneous of these, and shall make this speech of mine something new and variegated.

7. (*Thales gave even inanimate objects a soul*).

8. (*The continents Asia and Europe are called after two daughters of Ocean*).

9. (*The word 'tyrant' came into force later than Homer, who uses it to mean 'king'*).

10. (*Shortened form of 'deposit'*).

11. (*Lycurgus, the Spartan lawgiver, was warlike and experienced in many campaigns*).

12. (*Mamercus, brother of Stesichorus the poet, acquired a reputation for geometry*).

13. (*There are seven Hyades*).

14. (*The stepmother of Phrixus was called Gorgôpis*).

15. (*There was an Ephyra at Elis*).[1]

16. (*There are two sorts of envy, one right, when one envies the bad who are honoured, one wrong, when one envies the good.*

---

[1] *i.e.* as well as the Ephyra mentioned by Pindar, *Nem.* VII, who gave her name to a district of Corinth; and another unspecified. Cp. ch. 3 (Epimenides), Frg. 13,

Envious people have double sufferings: for their own troubles, and for other people's good fortune).

17. *('Calumny is a dread thing': no penalty is prescribed for it by law, yet it is theft, for it steals friendship, best of possessions; so that violence, bad as it is, is better than calumny, because it is not concealed).*

18. *(Homer came from Cymê).*

19. *(The name 'Of Hippias' without title of work, in a papyrus).*

Doubtful

20. (ARISTOTLE, *Poetics*, 1461a: *Examples of difficulties solved by accentuation in Homer: attributed to 'Hippias of Thasos', perhaps by confusion).*

21. (PROCLUS, *Commentary in Euclid: the quadratrices of Nicomedes and Hippias).*

87. ANTIPHÔN THE SOPHIST

ANTIPHÔN THE SOPHIST, believed to be of Athens, and to have lived in the latter half of the fifth century B.C.

Confusion has arisen over his identity: was he a different person from Antiphon the orator and Antiphon the tragedian? It is now generally believed that he was, and that his writings can be distinguished by difference of subject-matter and style.

If so, Antiphon the Sophist was a rhetorician, seer and interpreter of dreams. His chief work was called *Truth*; of this a portion has been discovered in an Oxyrhynchus papyrus. Other works were rhetorical essays *On Concord*, and on *The State*, or *The Statesman*; and a treatise on dream-interpretation. A treatise entitled *The Art of Freedom from Pain*, attributed to Antiphon the Orator, is now thought to be by Antiphon the Sophist.

1. (*From 'Truth'*): If you realise these things, you will know that there exists for it (*the mind*) no single thing of those things which the person who sees farthest sees with his vision, nor of those things which the person whose knowledge goes furthest knows with his mind.

2. In all men, the mind has the leadership of the body towards both health and disease and everything else.

3. (*From 'Truth'*): With unprepared mind. (*Unusual word for 'unprepared'*).

4. (*From 'Truth': word for 'unseen' used to mean 'things not seen but thought to be seen'*).

5. (*From 'Truth': word for 'unfelt' used to mean 'things not felt but thought to be felt'*).

6. (*Words for 'look through' and 'visible'*).

7. (*Words for 'sight' etc.*).

8. (*Words for 'smell'*).

9. Time is a thought or a measure, not a substance.

10. (*From 'Truth'*): Hence he (*God*) needs nothing and receives no addition from anywhere, but is infinite and lacking nothing.

11. (*From 'Truth': word for 'lack'*).

12. (*'Truth' ascribed to Antiphon the Orator*).

13. (ARISTOTLE, *Physics* 185a: *Antiphon's construction for the squaring of the circle by means of the inscription of triangles*).[1]

14. (*From 'Truth'*): Nature if stripped of her resources would have arranged many excellent things badly.

15. (*From 'Truth'*): If one buried a bed, and the rotting wood obtained life, it would become not a bed, but wood.

16. (*Usual word for 'extend': context unknown*).

(*From 'Truth', Book I*)
17. (*'Aphrodite' for 'sexual intercourse'*).

18. (*Word for 'gone over again from the beginning', of arguments, etc.*).

19. (*Word for 'proceed'*).

20. (*'Exchanges' used for 'combinations' or 'mixings'*).

21. (*Unusual word for 'desire'*).

(*From 'Truth', Book II*)
22. (*Word for 'everlastingness'*).

---

[1] Valueless. See *Companion*, pp. 396-7.

23. (*Word for 'the prevailing arrangement of the Whole'*).

24. (*Word for 'that which is still unarranged'*).

24a. (*Various uses of the word 'disposition'*).

25. By an eddy.

26. (*On the essence of the sun: it is a fire which feeds on the damp air round the earth, and its risings and settings are caused by the varying prevalence of the damp and the fiery elements*).

27. (*The moon has its own light, but the rays of the sun cause the parts round it to be dimmed*).

28. (*Eclipses of the moon are caused by the turning of its bowl*).

29. (*Hail*): When therefore in the air showers and contrary winds occur together, the water is then compressed and condensed to a large extent; and whichever of the colliding factors is overpowered is condensed and compressed by being squeezed together by the wind and its force.

30. (*The fire*) by heating the earth and melting it, makes it corrugated.

31. (*Word for earthquake*): Corrugation.

32. (*The sea is*) sweat, made salt (*by heating*).

33. (*Human skin*): Hide.

34. (*To give an analgesic for headache*): To stupefy.

35. (*Word for*) having blood.

36. That in which the embryo grows and is nourished is called 'membrane'.

37. Naval expedition (*context unknown*).

38. Abortion.

39. Mutilated things.

40. Dipping (*tempering*) of bronze and iron.

41. Skilled at maintaining life.

42. (*Word for*) weight.

43. (*Word for*) wealthy.

44. Justice, then, is not to transgress that which is the law of the city in which one is a citizen. A man therefore can best conduct himself in harmony with justice, if when in the company of witnesses he upholds the laws, and when alone without witnesses he upholds the edicts of nature. For the edicts of the laws are imposed artificially, but those of nature are compulsory. And the edicts of the laws are arrived at by consent, not by natural growth, whereas those of nature are not a matter of consent.

So, if the man who transgresses the legal code evades those who have agreed to these edicts, he avoids both disgrace and penalty; otherwise not. But if a man violates against possibility any of the laws which are implanted in nature, even if he evades all men's detection, the ill is no less, and even if all see, it is no greater. For he is not hurt on account of an opinion, but because of truth. The examination of these things is in general for this reason, that the majority of just acts according to law are prescribed contrary to nature. For there is legislation about the eyes, what they must see and what not; and about the ears, what they must hear and what not; and about the tongue, what it must speak and what not; and about the hands, what they must do and what not; and about the feet, where they must go and where not. Now the law's prohibitions are in no way more agreeable to nature and more akin than the law's injunctions. But life belongs to nature, and death too, and life for them is derived from advantages, and death from disadvantages. And the advantages laid down by the laws are chains upon nature, but those laid down by nature are free. So that the things which hurt, according to true reasoning, do not benefit nature more than those which delight; and things which grieve are not more advantageous than those which please; for things truly advantageous must not really harm, but must benefit. The naturally advantageous things from among these ...

(According to law, they are justified) who having suffered defend themselves and do not themselves begin action; and those who treat their parents well, even though their parents have treated them badly; and those who give the taking of an oath to others and do not themselves swear. Of these provisions, one could find many which are hostile to nature; and there is

in them the possibility of suffering more when one could suffer less; and enjoying less when one could enjoy more; and faring ill when one need not. Now if the person who adapted himself to these provisions received support from the laws, and those who did not, but who opposed them, received damage, obedience to the laws would not be without benefit; but as things are, it is obvious that for those who adapt themselves to these things the justice proceeding from law is not strong enough to help, seeing that first of all it allows him who suffers to suffer, and him who does, to do, and does not prevent the sufferer from suffering or the doer from doing. And if the case is brought up for punishment, there is no advantage peculiar to the sufferer rather than to the doer. For the sufferer must convince those who are to inflict the punishment, that he has suffered; and he needs the ability to win his case. And it is open to the doer to deny, by the same means ... and he can defend himself no less than the accuser can accuse, and persuasion is open to both parties, being a matter of technique. ...

We revere and honour those born of noble fathers, but those who are not born of noble houses we neither revere nor honour. In this we are, in our relations with one another, like barbarians, since we are all by nature born the same in every way, both barbarians and Hellenes. And it is open to all men to observe the laws of nature, which are compulsory. Similarly all of these things can be acquired by all, and in none of these things is any of us distinguished as barbarian or Hellene. We all breathe into the air through mouth and nostrils, and we all eat with hands. ...

(From another book of 'Truth')

If justice were taken seriously, then witnessing the truth among one another is considered just, and useful no less for men's business affairs. But he who does this is not just, since not to wrong anyone unless wronged oneself is just; for it is inevitable for the witness, even if he witnesses to the truth, nevertheless to wrong another in some way, and at the same time himself be wronged later, because of what he said; in that because of the evidence given by him, the person witnessed against is condemned, and loses either money or his life, through someone to whom he does no wrong. Therein therefore he wrongs the man against whom he gives evidence, in that he wrongs someone who did him no wrong; and he himself is wronged by the man against whom he gave evidence, because he is hated by him for having given truthful evidence. And (*he is wronged*) not only by this hatred, but also because he must for the whole of his life be on his guard against the man against whom he gave evidence; for he has an enemy such that he will say or do him any harm in his power. Indeed, these are clearly no small wrongs which he himself suffers and which he inflicts; for these cannot be just, nor can the demand to do no wrong (*if one is not wronged?*) But it is inevitable that either both are just or both unjust. It is clear, also, that to judge, give judgement, and arbitrate for a settlement are not just; for that which helps some, hurts others; and in this case, those who are benefited are not wronged, but those who are injured are wronged. . . .

44a. (PHILOSTRATUS: *The speech 'On behalf of Concord' is his most brilliant, being full of apophthegms, dignified in style, adorned with poetical terms, and smoothly-flowing*).

(*Names of tribes*)
45. Shadowfeet.

46. Longheads.

47. (*Troglodytes*). Dwellers underground.

48. Man, who, they say, is the most divine of all animals.

49. Now let life proceed, and let him desire marriage and a wife. This day, this night begin a new destiny; for marriage is a great contest for mankind. If the woman turns out to be incompatible, what can one do about the disaster? Divorce is difficult: it means to make enemies of friends, who have the same thoughts, the same breath, and had been valued and had regarded one with esteem. And it is hard if one gets such a possession, that is, if when thinking to get pleasure, one brings home pain.

However, not to speak of malevolence: let us assume the utmost compatibility. What is pleasanter to a man than a wife after his own heart? What is sweeter, especially to a young man? But in the very pleasure lies near at hand the pain; pleasures do not come alone, but are attended by griefs and troubles. Olympic and Pythian victories and all pleasures are apt to be won by great pains. Honours, prizes, delights, which God has given to men, depend necessarily on great toils and exertions. For my part, if I had another body which was as much trouble to me as I am to myself, I could not live, so great is the trouble I give myself for the sake of health, the acquisition of a livelihood, and for fame, respectability, glory and a good reputation. What then, if I acquired another body which was as much trouble? Is it not clear that a wife, if she is to his mind, gives her husband no less cause for love and pain than he does to himself, for the health of two bodies, the acquisition of two livelihoods, and for respectability and honour? Suppose children are born: then all is full of anxiety, and the youthful spring goes out of the mind, and the countenance is no longer the same.

50. Life is like a day-long watch, and the length of life is like one day, as it were, on which having seen the light we pass on our trust to the next generation.

51. The whole of life is wonderfully open to complaint, my friend; it has nothing remarkable, great or noble, but all is petty, feeble, brief-lasting, and mingled with sorrows.

52. It is not possible to rearrange one's (*past*) life, like pieces on a draught-board.

53. Those who work and save and suffer and lay money by enjoy the sort of pleasure one can imagine. But when they take away from it and use it, they suffer pain as if tearing off their own flesh.

53a. There are some who do not live the present life, but prepare with great diligence as if they were going to live another life, not the present one. Meanwhile time, being neglected, deserts them.

54. There is a story that a man seeing another man earning much money begged him to lend him a sum at interest. The other refused; and being of a mistrustful nature, unwilling to help anyone, he carried it off and hid it somewhere. Another man, observing him, filched it. Later, the man who had hidden it returning, could not find it; and being very grieved at the disaster — especially that he had not lent to the man who had

asked him, because then it would have been safe and would have earned increment — he went to see the man who had asked for a loan, and bewailed his misfortune, saying that he had done wrong and was sorry not to have granted his request but to have refused it, as his money was completely lost. The other man told him to hide a stone in the same place, and think of his money as his and not lost: 'For even when you had it you completely failed to use it; so that now too you can think you have lost nothing.' For when a person has not used and will not use anything, it makes no difference to him either whether he has it or not. For when God does not wish to give a man complete good fortune — when he has given him material wealth but made him poor in right thinking — in taking away one he has deprived him of both.

55. To hesitate where there is no place for hesitation.

56. He is cowardly who is bold in speech concerning absent and future dangers, and hurries on in resolve, but shrinks back when the fact is upon him.

57. 'Illness is a holiday for cowards',[1] for they do not march into action.

58. Whoever, when going against his neighbour with the intention of harming him, is afraid lest by failing to achieve his wishes he may get what he does not wish, is wiser. For his fear means hesitation, and his hesitation means an interval in which often his mind is deflected from his purpose. There can be no reversal of a thing that has happened: it is possible only for what is in the future not to happen. Whoever thinks he will illtreat his neighbours and not suffer himself is unwise. Hopes are not altogether a good thing; such hopes have flung down many into intolerable disaster, and what they thought to inflict on their neighbours, they have suffered themselves for all to see. Prudence in another man can be judged correctly by no one more than he who fortifies his soul against immediate pleasures and can conquer himself. But whoever wishes to gratify his soul immediately, wishes the worse instead of the better.

59. Whoever has not desired or touched the base and the

---

[1] A proverb.

bad, is not self-restrained; for there is nothing over which he has gained the mastery and proved himself well-behaved. .

60. The first thing, I believe, for mankind is education. For whenever anyone does the beginning of anything correctly, it is likely that the end also will be right. As one sows, so can one expect to reap. And if in a young body one sows a noble education, this lives and flourishes through the whole of his life, and neither rain nor drought destroys it.

61. Nothing is worse for mankind than anarchy. Hence our forefathers instilled obedience into their children, so that when grown up they might not be overcome by any great change (*of fortune*).

62. One's character must necessarily grow like that with which one spends the greater part of the day.

63. When they understand the arrangement, they listen.

(*From 'On Concord'; context unknown*).
64. New friendships are close, but old ones are closer.

65. Many who have friends do not know it, but choose as companions admirers of their wealth and flatterers of their good fortune.

66. The care of old age is like the care of children. —

(*Words from 'On Concord'*)
67. Not to be seen.

67a. Manhood.

68. Bivouacking (*for 'sleeping'*).

69. Starting-place (*metaphor from games, for 'beginning'*).

70. Manageable (*metaphor from driving horses*).

71. Deceptions.

(*From 'The Statesman'*)
72. Disobedience to the government.

73. When anyone has 'breakfasted away' his own or his friends' property. . . .

74. One who readily contributes (*his share*).

75. Doubling and halving.

76. Do not be called a tippler, and appear to neglect your affairs under the influence of wine.

From an unspecified writing
77. To spend the most costly commodity, time.

(*From 'On the Interpretation of Dreams'*)
78. Cuttle-fish (*signifies escape*).

79. (CICERO: *Antiphon's explanations of many trivial dreams are artificial, not natural*).

80. (*ib.: Examples of Antiphon's interpretations of dreams: an Olympic competitor dreams that he is driving a four-horse chariot; the interpreter says 'You will win', but Antiphon says 'You will lose, because four have run before you'. Another competitor dreams that he is an eagle; this is thought to mean victory, but Antiphon says 'You will lose', because the eagle pursues other birds and so comes after*).

81. (SENECA: *Junius Otho published four books on 'Specious Pleas',*[1] *which were sometimes ascribed to Antiphon because there was so much about dreams in them*).

81a. (MELAMPUS *on Twitchings: If the right eye twitches, this, according to Phêmonoê, the Egyptians and Antiphon, means that one will overcome one's enemies. If the upper eyelid twitches, this means gain; according to Antiphon, health and success, but in a slave, treachery; for a widow, a journey*).

82-117. (*Fragments, mostly single words, which may come from the Sophist or the Orator*).

118. (*Title: 'On Farming': probably 'Antiphon' here should read 'Androtion'*).

88. CRITIAS OF ATHENS

CRITIAS of ATHENS lived from about 480 B.C. to 403 B.C.

He wrote in verse and prose. His verse works included a poem in hexameters on the poets; elegiacs on inventions, on *Constitutions*, and other subjects; experimental verses; and plays. He also wrote in prose on *Constitutions*; and his other prose works included *Conversations, Aphor-*

---

[1] *Colores*, a technical term in rhetoric: Quintilian, IV. ii. 88.

isms, and various speeches or essays now lost. He was 'a philosopher among amateurs, an amateur among philosophers'.

1. (*Hexameters: On Anacreon*): ... And he who once wove poems for women's song, Anacreon, whom Teos gave to Greece, the stimulator of banquets, the deceiver of women, the antagonist of flutes, lover of the lyre, sweet, free from pain. Never shall love of thee grow old, or die, so long as the boy serves the water mixed with wine, from left to right, and female choirs ply the dance all night long, and the bowl, the daughter of bronze, sits on the top of the Cottabos, struck by the drops of Bacchus!

2. (*Elegiacs*): The Cottabos is from Sicily, a noble art, which we set up as a target for the shots of wine-lees; also the wagon is Sicilian, best in beauty and magnificence ... The throne is Thessalian, the most luxurious seat for the limbs. Miletus, and Chios, island-state of Oenopion, have the greatest works of art in sleeping-beds. The Etruscan gold-wrought goblet is the best, and all bronze which adorns the home for any purpose. The Phoenicians invented writing, aid to thought. Thebes first put together the chariot-seat, and the Carians, curators of the sea, the ships that carry merchandise. But the potter's wheel, and the child of earth and oven, glorious pottery, useful household ware, was invented by her who set up the trophy at Marathon.

3. (*Orpheus invented the dactylic hexameter*).

4. (*One hexameter and one iambic line: To Alcibiades*): Now I will crown the Athenian, son of Cleinias, Alcibiades, hymning him in new ways; for it was not possible to fit his name into elegy. Now it will lie in iambics not unmetrically.

5. (*The same*): The resolution which brought you back, I said it before all, and drafted it, and completed this act. The seal of my tongue lies upon this (*word*).

(*'Constitutions' in metre: The Constitution of the Spartans*)
6. This custom too is fixed at Sparta, to drink always the same beaker of wine, and not to drink healths, giving back one's cup and calling on a name, nor to hand it to the right round the circle of the company. . . .
The Lydian hand, the Asiatic, devised the large vessels, and

the custom of passing (*the cup*) to the right in drinking healths, and calling on a name to which one wishes to drink. Then, from so much drinking, they loosen their tongues in base speech, and enfeeble their body; a dim cloud settles on the eye, forgetfulness dissolves memory from the thoughts, and the mind totters. Slaves have uncontrolled natures. Expense that wears away the house falls on it. But the Spartan youths drink only so much as to lead the thoughts of all towards cheerful hope, and friendly speech, and moderate laughter. This kind of drinking is good for the body, the mind and the property; it is well fitted for the works of love and for song, the harbour of cares, and for health, most delightful of all goddesses for mortals, and Moderation, neighbour of piety ... For the drinking of healths beyond the right measure brings, after joy, enduring pain. But the Spartan way of life is balanced — to be able to eat and drink conformably with thought and work. There is no day set apart for excessive drinking (*at Sparta*).

7. Chilon, a Spartan, was the author of 'Nothing too much'; all that is good is attached to 'Right Season'.

8. (*I would wish for*) the wealth of the Scopadae, the magnanimity of Cimon, the victories of Arcesilas of Sparta.

9. More men are good through habit than through character.[1]

Plays[2]
10. (*Of the plays attributed to Euripides, three are spurious: 'Tennês', 'Rhadamanthys', 'Peirithôus'*).

(*From 'Tennês'*)
11. (*Tennês: eponymous hero of Tenedos*).

12. Alas! Nothing is just in the present generation.

(*From 'Rhadamanthys'*)
12a. (*End of hypothesis discovered at Oxyrhynchus*).

13. Nobody will take us away ...

14. ... Who live in Euboea, neighbouring State ...

---

[1] Cp. Democritus, Frg. 242.
[2] See *Companion*, pp. 411-12, for reasons for attributing these plays to Critias.

15. Our loves in life are of every kind. One man longs to have nobility, another cares nothing for this, but wishes to be called the master of many possessions in his halls. Another is pleased to speak what is utterly unsound from his mind and to persuade his neighbours with wicked boldness. Others seek shameful gains from mortals rather than honour. But I wish to win none of these: I would choose to have a reputation of fair fame.

(*From 'Peirithôus'*)
15a. (*New fragments discovered at Oxyrhynchus: 'Peirithôus'*):
(*On Ixion*): Divine madness sent Atê. He had a cloud for wife and sowed a rumour full of Hybris among the Thessalians, that he had had intercourse with the daughter of Cronos. For such boasts he paid penalty to the gods, being whirled round on the wheel of madness, driven by a gadfly, unknown to men. Nor did a tomb cover him, but he was torn asunder by the (?) of the North Winds: my father, having sinned against the gods.

(*Dialogue between Heracles and Theseus*)
Theseus I must stay: I cannot betray a comrade.
Heracl. You speak worthily of yourself and Athens, for you always help the unfortunate. It is disgraceful to me to have an excuse to go home. For how do you think Eurystheus would rejoice if he heard that I had helped you in this, to be able to say that the toil had been undergone in vain?
Theseus Well, for what you wish you have everywhere my goodwill, not under compulsion but freely, (*goodwill*) hostile to foes, kindly to friends. . . .
(*The rest is too much mutilated for restoration*).

16. (*Aeacus in Hades, to Heracles*): Ha, what is this? I see someone hurrying thither with confident mind. Tell me truly, stranger, who are you who approach these regions, and for what reason?

(*Heracles replies*): I have no hesitation in disclosing the whole tale. My native land is Argos, my name is Heracles, I am the son of Zeus, father of all the gods; for Zeus came to my mother's marriage-bed, as is said in truth. I come here perforce, obeying the commands of Eurystheus, who sent me to fetch the hound of hell alive to the gates of Mycenae, and he thought that in this he had invented a task impossible for me to fulfil. On this quest I have travelled round to the remote regions of all Europe and Asia.

17. (*Mention of the Plêmochoê, earthenware vessel used on the last day of the Eleusinian Mysteries*).
Chorus: In order that we may pour forth these vessels into the earthy chasm.

18. Time, unwearying and full, with ever-flowing stream, self-begetting; and the Twin Bears with swift-moving wings, who guard the Pole of Atlas.

19. (*I call on*) thee, the self-made, who hast woven the nature of all things in the aetherial whirl, round whom Light, and dusky Night with shimmering colour, and the innumerable throng of the stars, for ever dance.

20. (*Theseus-is*) bound in the unwrought fetters of honour.

21. He spoke with mind not untrained who first threw out the new saying that Fortune is the ally of sensible men.

22. A good character is more securely based than law; for no orator can ever overturn it, whereas he can upset the latter with speech and often maim it.

23. Is it not better not to live than to live miserably?

24. (*Usually attributed to Euripides*)[1] Fame reveals the good man even in the hollows of the earth.

No, but Hades received me when still living.

Aphidnus, son of Earth who has no mother.

(*From 'Sisyphus', satyric play*)
25. There was a time when the life of men was unordered, bestial and the slave of force, when there was no reward for the virtuous and no punishment for the wicked. Then, I think, men devised retributory laws, in order that Justice might be dictator and have arrogance as its slave, and if anyone sinned, he was punished. Then, when the laws forbade them to commit open crimes of violence, and they began to do them in

---

[1] Attribution to Critias by Welcker and Wilamowitz; the latter gives to Critias Eur. *Frg. inc.* 964 also (*Vors.* Vol. II, 14, 5).

secret, a wise and clever man invented fear (*of the gods*) for mortals, that there might be some means of frightening the wicked, even if they do anything or say or think it in secret. Hence he introduced the Divine (*religion*), saying that there is a God flourishing with immortal life, hearing and seeing with his mind, and thinking of everything and caring about these things, and having divine nature, who will hear everything said among mortals, and will be able to see all that is done. And even if you plan anything evil in secret, you will not escape the gods in this; for they have surpassing intelligence. In saying these words, he introduced the pleasantest of teachings, covering up the truth with a false theory; and he said that the gods dwelt there where he could most frighten men by saying it, whence he knew that fears exist for mortals and rewards for the hard life: in the upper periphery, where they saw lightnings and heard the dread rumblings of thunder, and the starry-faced body of heaven, the beautiful embroidery of Time the skilled craftsman, whence come forth the bright mass of the sun, and the wet shower upon the earth. With such fears did he surround mankind, through which he well established the deity with his argument, and in a fitting place, and quenched lawlessness among men . . . Thus, I think, for the first time did someone persuade mortals to believe in a race of deities.

(From unspecified dramas)
26. After the shadow, Time grows old most speedily.

27. Whoever in his dealings with his friends does all according to their pleasure is creating an immediate pleasure which will turn to future enmity.

28. It is terrible when one who is not wise thinks himself so.

29. Is it better to have rich stupidity rather than wise poverty as one's companion in the house?

Prose fragments
30. (*Title:* 'Constitution of the Athenians').

31. (*From* 'Constitution of the Thessalians'): The Thessalians are agreed to have become the richest of the Greeks in their clothes and way of life: by which they became the cause of the Persian invasion, because the latter envied them their luxury and expenditure.

(From 'Constitution of the Spartans'):

32.   I begin with birth: how can a man become physically best and strongest? — If the father takes exercise and eats well and hardens himself, and the mother of the future child is physically strong and takes exercise.

33.   The Chian and Thasian drink from big beakers, handing (*them*) to the right, the Attic from small ones, handing to the right; the Thessalian pledges big cups to whomever he wishes; but the Spartans each drink the cup beside them, and the wine-bearer pours in just so much as each will drink.

34.   Apart from these things, (*to come to*) the smallest matters of daily life: Spartan shoes are the best, their cloaks the pleasantest and most convenient to wear; the Spartan goblet is the most suitable for war and the easiest to carry in one's wallet. The reason why it is best is: the soldier is often obliged to drink from water that is not pure; therefore in the first place the drink is not too clearly visible; and second, it has an incurving rim which catches impurities.

35.   (*Comparison of Spartan household furniture with the Milesian bed and chair, and the Chian bed, and the Rhêneian table*).

36.   (*The early Spartans*) used to leap into the air, and before descending, made many movements of their feet, which they called 'to dance the tong-dance'.

37.   (*Spartiates and Helots: the distinction between slave and free is greatest in Sparta*): Because of mistrust, the Spartiate at home takes the handles off their (*the Helots'*) shields. Not being able to do this in war, because of the frequent need for speedy use, he goes round always carrying his spear, thinking to overcome the Helot with it if he tries separate mutiny with the shield only. They have also devised bolts, which they believe to be strong enough to withstand any attack from the Helots.

38.   (*From an unspecified 'Constitution': reference to 'trousers' and 'breeches'*).

39.   (*From his 'Aphorisms'*) . . . Neither what he perceives with the rest of his body, nor what he knows with his mind.
   Men know (*this*) who are accustomed to be healthy in mind.

(From 'Conversations'):

40. If you yourself would practise in order to become sufficiently able in mind, you would thus least be wronged by them (*i.e. the sense-perceptions?*).

41. (*Word for 'impulse'*).

41a. (PLATO, *Charmides* 161B): Self-restraint is to mind one's own business.

42. (*From 'On the Nature of Love', or 'of the Virtues'*): He is bad-tempered who is vexed over trifles, and over big things either more than other men, or for a longer time.

43. (*Title: 'Popular Prooemia'*).

(From unspecified prose works)

44. (*Critias, blaming Archilochus for vilifying himself, says*): Otherwise, if he had not published this view of himself in Greece, we should not have known either that he was the son of Enîpô, a slave-woman, nor that he left Paros because of poverty and destitution and went to Thasos, nor that when there he was on bad terms with the inhabitants, nor that he vilified friends and foes equally. Moreover, we would not have known that he was an adulterer, nor lustful and violent, if we had not learnt it from him, and — most disgraceful of all — that he threw away his shield. So that Archilochus was not a good witness for himself, leaving behind such a reputation and such a name.

45. (*Before Themistocles took up politics, he had an inheritance of three talents; when he was banished and his property confiscated, he was found to have one hundred talents. So too Cleon had nothing of his own before he entered politics, but afterwards he left behind a property of fifty talents*).

46, 47. (*Comparison of Critias' style with that of Xenophon*).

48. A feminine form is the greatest beauty in men; in women, the opposite.

49. Nothing is certain, except that having been born we die, and that in life one cannot avoid disaster.

50. (*Homer's father was a river*).

51. The Pythian contest (*quoted to show word-order*).

52. (*After the earthquake at Sparta, Cimon persuaded the Athenians to send them help*).

Separate words
53. See through.

54. Speaker.

55. Quickhanded.

56. Dirtiness.

57. Prosode ('*song sung to the lyre*').

58. Two-drachma men.

59. To drink beaker after beaker.

60. Purchase of fish. To buy fish. To watch the price of fish.

61. False witnesses.

62. To be scattered.

63. So far as depends on courage.

64. Cloaksellers.

65. Leggings.

66. Ring-engravers.

67. Dealer in music-strings.

68. Perfumier.

69. Hairnet-maker.

70. Dealers in brass, iron, vegetables, cheese, emetics, tow, wool, incense, roots, silphium, green-groceries, utensils; seed-gatherer, seedsman; sellers of pots, drugs, weapons, pictures, birds.

71. Acquit. Serve as dicast throughout.

72. Towndweller.

73. Shrewdness.

74. (*Graeco-Syrian Maxims: the name is uncertain, and the matter has nothing in common with the work of Critias*).

75. (PLATO, *Republic* 368A: '*Glaucon's admirer*', *who wrote elegiac verses in praise of 'the sons of Ariston', may be Critias*).

89. THE ANONYMOUS WRITER QUOTED BY IAMBLICHUS

THE ANONYMOUS WRITER QUOTED BY IAMBLICHUS

An ethico-political essay in literary Attic, believed to belong to the time of the Peloponnesian War.

It deals with success; the factors necessary for its achievement (natural endowment, good will, industry, an early start); how to use success when attained; the need for self-control, which means being superior to money but generous with soul (life); the disadvantages of self-aggrandizement, and the advantages of obedience to law; the evil of tyranny, which arises from lawlessness.

90. TWOFOLD ARGUMENTS (DEBATES)

TWOFOLD ARGUMENTS (DEBATES)

An anonymous sophistical essay written in literary Doric after the end of the Peloponnesian War, and setting out to show that there are two sides to every question.

' Examples: good and bad, honourable and dishonourable, just and unjust, true and false are (1) the same, (2) not the same. Madmen and sane, wise and ignorant (1) do and say the same things, (2) do not. Wisdom and virtue can, or cannot, be taught. Offices should not be awarded by lot. It belongs to the same man to be politician, speaker, scientist.

Rules are given for aiding memory, most useful of powers.

DATE DUE

OC 31 '83		
NO 14 '83		
NO 1 2 '86		
SE 27 '88		
GAYLORD		PRINTED IN U.S.A.